Employee Coaching

For

Business Success

Building a High Performance Work Culture

Donna Lynn Price

Employee Coaching For Business Success

Building a High Performance Work Culture

By Donna Lynn Price

ISBN-13: 978-1492717744

ISBN-10: 1492717746

Other Books by Donna Lynn Price

* How to Market Your Dream Business To Create Financial Freedom
* Launching Your Dreams: Stop Day Dreaming and Live Your Vision
* Coaching Staff for Success
* Bizology.Biz: The Science of Building a Thriving Business

Dedication

Dedicated to the business leaders, managers and supervisors that have the courage to embark on a new approach, to work to create better workplaces for employees, managers, owners and customers.

Content

Acknowledgments

I have to thank the many people that I have worked with over the years; from colleagues to staff I supervised, to leaders that I learned from. Each has contributed to who I am and where I have ended up as a leader and consultant. Without the teachings I have received from many others this book would not be. Thank you.

Introduction

This book is a culmination of work, experience, training and observation. As a manager for many years I worked to coach staff before we called it coaching. And at times I micro managed, disciplined and did not use the best approaches that we teach people to use now. We all worked to do our best in the settings we were in, with the teachers we had.

Now, as a consultant and coach, I work to help people to create better workplaces for themselves and their employees. That has been my goal in each place that I have worked, whether it was realized or not. I have always felt that people should have good working environments, with good supervisors that treated them fairly, with respect and care and that as a result the business would thrive.

It is challenging to supervise people. People dynamics are ever changing and never totally predictable. People bring their own histories and backgrounds to the table. As the manager, you never know exactly what that will mean for your team. Using a coaching approach to working with staff gives you as the manager the skills to navigate the many different staff you will encounter and to assist them in being as successful as possible. Employee Coaching for Business Success is about you and your business being the best it can be, with a staff that is motivated, performance focused and pretty happy!

The benefits to you and your organization in shifting the environment to one of coaching, collaboration and high performance is tremendous. You end up creating a company that people want to work for! One that is excellent in services, customer retention and high quality products. Your company shines both inside and out. The energy is palpable and people know it.

There are challenges along the way but the results are fun! The journey is worth taking and there are roses to smell along the way. You will be amazed at the staff that you have that stay on board and join you.

To Your Success!

Donna Lynn Price

Chapter 1

Moving From Micro Management to Coaching

Empowering Produces Results

The leader that micro manages his or her team, might be sacrificing bottom line results and team performance for that control. Control is hard to give up when you are the leader or manager. You just have that feeling that others won't do it as well as you, or that if you don't make every decision, mistakes will be made. To some extent that is true. When you think back to your own journey you can probably find a few mistakes that you made along the way. They were lessons that have guided your ultimate success. Empowering your staff gives them responsibility and opens up the possibilities of mistakes and new lessons. Part of the leader's responsibility is training staff to take on responsibility. The other part is letting go of the micro level control and empowering staff to do things, perhaps differently than you would and perhaps better!

When leaders have to have control over each detail they slow operations down, they demoralize the staff and decrease performance. Staff Have ideas, insights into the day to day operations of companies. They can anticipate problems and see ways to overcome them. They know the tasks that need to get done and can schedule those to fit into the team's workload more effectively. When leaders don't empower their staff the results are poorer. But the results are even direr than that. Demoralized staff doesn't stay forever. They look for other options. They seek positions where there are opportunities for growth and increased responsibility.

The micro manger needs to do some self-reflection to identify why they need control. What is holding them back from letting their staff shine and take the lead? Often it is their own confidence and the need to recognition. Confident and self-assured leaders can give over the reins to their staff.

Benefits of Empowered Employees

Empowering employees can have multiple positive benefits to the workplace. Employees can take the lead on projects and tasks and free up the manager or leader to do other things. The leader often has the responsibility of growing the company. When they tie themselves up in the day to day operations they remove themselves from this important task. Growing the company, getting out and acquiring new projects, new clients and visioning greater success are all part of being the CEO or leader. Employees can take on the day to day operations of organizations.

Empowering employees is good for morale. When managers have to control every aspect of an employee's work it is demoralizing to the employee. When staff make suggestions or put forth ideas and they are never accepted or considered, or have to be the idea of the manger or leader, then employees stop making suggestions. Staffs do not work for pay alone. Work conditions play a major role in staff satisfaction and performance. When staff are in a situation where they have little control, are not acknowledged for their work or ideas then their performance suffers. The results for the team or the company are negative. Turn-over increases and the costs to organization are impacted.

Empowering means giving up some control, but does not mean that the organization runs wild. Staffs have great ideas. It is gold. They see ways to improve operations, get things done faster, easier for less cost. The misconception of the micro manager is that only they care about the company. When true leaders share their vision and passion for the company, employees can embrace that vision and passion as well. When that leader then empowers the employees to do great work, results can soar.

As the leader or CEO you can set up communication systems that empower employees and at the same time keep you informed and in the loop. But you do need to follow through and let employees make

decisions and not take back all control when you are informed of staff decisions.

Empowering instead of micro managing will result in better organizational results and free you, the leader up to further grow the organization.

Chapter 2

Leadership:
The Essentials of Effective
Leadership

Leaders model leadership with their actions

In history students learn about the activities, good and bad, that individual historians label as a good leader and leadership. We study their personalities to extract the qualities required for leadership. Experts argue whether leaders are made or born. I think it's some of both, based on situations and the individual. You can teach someone to lead but they must have the desire and certain personality or character traits to be effective and a high quality leader. Others are never taught leadership but in a situation that calls for leadership they emerge as a natural leader.

Leaders are sometimes defined as revolutionaries. During times of conflict or change one individual usually stands out. That person has the ability to motivate individuals to fight for something that is difficult. Martin Luther King Jr. is an example of a leader involved in a social cause that required charismatic leadership, courage and the ability to inspire people. War also requires a leader. The absence of a leader in situations like these could dramatically change the outcomes.

In business, the roles of leader and manager are somewhat intertwined.

"Leader" usually implies a broad view, the person at the top, the visionary. The buck stops here usually means the leader is the one ultimately responsible for the success or failure of a given mission. Leaders utilize managers to help them complete their tasks. The "managers" are often not the "leader" but rather the implementer and at the same time they are expected to lead, thus the mixture of manager and leader.

The current world situation calls for strong leadership. Recent changes in technology, economics, communication and social issues create problems that individuals and companies are struggling to deal with. It seems as if there's a whole new arena of leaders emerging. Bookstores offer numerous viewpoints by individuals promoting what they believe

it takes to successfully lead a company. Some of these are excellent resources. But, is there a magic formula? Can someone learn to lead by reading a book? And yet, here you are reading my book and I hope it gives you the insights and learning for your leadership journey.

Leadership is a lifelong learning journey. Developing the skills of leadership requires lifelong learning. Leaders need to be self-reflective and have the ability to continuously assess their skills and their gaps. Leadership development and executive coaching support leaders in mastering the gaps.

Many of the qualities of successful leaders from the past are still essential today.

Some things like integrity never change. Perhaps some individuals we looked up to as leaders forgot or disregarded qualities such as character. Society is fed up with immoral living, dishonesty and selfishness of many of today's business leaders. Emerging leaders need to restore the "good name" formerly associated with leadership, as well as embrace the changes in our current global society.

Experts have different opinions on what makes a good leader. Most people would agree there are certain characteristics that all good leaders must possess.

The following qualities I believe are essential for effective leaders. They are not necessarily in order of importance.

Passion

All strong leaders have passion.

They are totally committed to and sold on their cause. The end goal or result is the over driving force in their life. They eat, breath and sleep

this; sometimes to excess. Driven to succeed they also have the ability to ignite excitement in others. Without passion they could not enlist followers. Sometimes this is confused with enthusiasm or charisma. Having passion can lead to those qualities but they are not requirements. Mother Teresa was not known for her enthusiasm, but for her passion, as passion can drive a cause.

Vision

Leaders have vision.

They look beyond today and see the big picture. Not content with how things are now they see something better in the future. A good leader is realistic about current circumstances but they don't feel trapped. Their desire to succeed or make things better drives them to find ways to make this happen. Great leaders are the visionaries. They envision the future and share their vision. Within the vision is passion.

Self-Confidence

Leaders possess self-confidence.

They've had past success, they know what they're capable of and most of all they understand the importance of never giving up. If they fail they continue trying until they succeed. Philosophers believe that thinking you can do something is half the battle. If you don't think you can do something you probably will not even try. A confident leader inspires their followers to believe in themselves.

Integrity

A good leader is truthful and dependable.

Followers of leaders with integrity do not have to wonder if something their leader said is true – they know it is true. This is based on past behavior and reputation of the leader. Lies and deceitful behavior eventually surface. If this happens individuals are reluctant to follow someone they do not trust. Sometimes a leader doesn't reveal all they know and they might even dress something up due to sensitive issues but integrity is buried deep in their essence. They don't look for dishonest ways to do something or how to cheat the system, for example.

Humble

> *Great leaders are humble.*

They do not feel they are better than anyone else. They are willing to do everything they ask their followers to do. A leader recognizes the importance of teamwork and gives credit to others. It's not their success but the team's success. They don't boast or brag and sometimes even have difficulty taking credit. Sometimes humility is incorrectly defined as weakness. Jesus, washing the feet of his disciples and other acts he did, is a great example of humbleness. Leaders that take credit from others are looked down upon and respect is lost.

Knowledge

> *A leader must possess the knowledge required to complete their mission.*

Leaders are usually avid readers, life-long students, and view every situation as an opportunity to learn more. Knowledge and education are not the same. Sometimes individuals with advanced learning possess little knowledge. Knowledge is like advanced common sense. Much of it comes from life experience. A leader's knowledge could be defined as

wisdom. Wisdom is not only having knowledge but knowing how to use it in the most effective way. As the leader continues to learn, reflect and observe they grow their personal reserve of wisdom.

Think Outside The Box

Leaders know that things and life constantly change.

Leaders know that clinging to current methods and refusing to consider all possibilities prevents growth and eventually leads to stagnation. Individuals who think outside the box know their ideas are not always right therefore they seek input from others. By sharing ideas and gaining additional input and creativity, great ideas are born. Such out of the box thinking sometimes leads to radical change. Then the next challenge of leadership may arise: resistance to change. People resist change especially something drastic that affects them personally. Doing things like everyone else makes you "normal". Breaking away from the status quo makes you "different". Good leaders do not follow the crowd but rather search for the best way to complete their mission.

Accept Failure

Leaders know they do not always make the right decision but that mistakes are opportunities for learning.

They admit their mistakes without making excuses. Mistakes for them are opportunities to learn. They don't give up or wallow in self-pity. By admitting mistakes a leader reveals their humility. Though we want our leaders to be like super heroes, we also want them to be human and humble.

Be Generous

Your generosity builds loyalty.

Generosity of time, benefits, wages, perks, working conditions and yourself. Greed of organizations, leaders or owners does not help their success. Treating staff fairly, and with generosity assists in building the rapport and success that you as the leader want. It is part of building a great place for people to work.

Much of my professional work experience was in the non-profit sector. Front line staffs in non-profits often have very demanding jobs for low wages. As a manager, I worked to make working conditions and wages fair and sustainable. If we worked people so hard that they had little personal time and little money they typically didn't stay very long. As an organization we spent a great deal of time and money recruiting and training new staff. We could have shifted that resource to pay fair wages and had long term staff which would have benefited the organization and the clients we served.

As an employer, being fair is not just the right thing to do, but it builds trust, loyalty and a more effective team.

Courage

Leadership Takes Courage.

With courage, passion, vision, integrity and humbleness a great leader can climb mountains. Their businesses and the people that work with them excel and greatness is attained, not for the purpose of greatness but for the accomplishment of vision and mission. Their goal is clear and compelling and being such their teams work with them to achieve it. Great leadership remains unchanged decade to decade, century to

century, and perhaps bad leadership remains unchanged as well. But it is with great leadership that we continue to thrive and build great companies, communities and ultimately the world.

> *When leaders lead with courage, organizations thrive.*

Leaders must possess essentials of good character. The real world skills of leadership can be learned through a process of assessment, training, practice and refinement. Coaches can be effective partners in this ongoing process.

Chapter 3

Motivating Your Staff

Creating feelings that inspire.

Leadership and motivation are also closely related. A person can motivate without being a leader. But all leaders motivate, they create feelings in everyone they meet. The resulting motivation can be positive or negative. Leaders often say they like everything about their job except for managing people and if they leave their management jobs for something else, they do not miss the headaches that come with managing others. I've had many jobs and many leaders. In my opinion most of my leaders were not qualified to manage. It's difficult for a bad manager to motivate their staff in a positive way. Good leaders on the other hand usually have a positive effect on their employees.

It takes a while to figure out the work environment. Sometimes I think it helps to throw all your assumptions out the window. Things do not always make sense at work. The best management candidates do not always get the job. Sometimes unqualified individuals are put in positions of authority. It is true that many individuals reach their level of incompetence, go a little higher, and then settle in a position where they neither grow nor leave. There's a good chance you are more qualified to manage than your boss.

Motivation can be positive or negative. Experts say that children often do things with negative consequences just to get attention. Many leaders excel in creating negative motivation. Employees work for different reasons. They put up with a lot of stuff because they need the money, the benefits or the job. The manager that doesn't motivate their employees in a positive way probably has a team of unhappy employees. Unhappy employees produce lower results for their companies than engaged, empowered and happy employees. No one likes going to work if they are belittled, put down and called inadequate. Eventually unhappy employees leave or burnout.

Leading others is one of the most difficult jobs an individual ever does. I always thought it was difficult enough to manage myself, why would I want to lead others?

Local bookstores and the Internet offer numerous books on how to be an effective manager or leader, plus the specific topic of motivation. Reading about the successful techniques of others is an excellent way to learn. Along with the serious books there's also a large collection of comic type books portraying humor in work situations. The target of most jokes is the boss, often portrayed as incompetent and disliked. You can even learn something from a bad boss.

In the working environment there are many individuals that motivate employees. Maybe it's the parking lot attendant, the clerk in the mail room, the co-worker who shares your work space or a customer you talk to by phone. To a certain extent you motivate everyone you come in contact with and everyone is motivated by you. When you break motivation down to its simplest form it actually means how something or someone makes you feel. This can be good, bad or neutral. In most business environments leaders are expected to motivate the individuals they manage though it's not always written in the job description.

Sometimes I think we make managing others more complicated than it has to be. The leader who treats others the way they like to be treated is off to a good start. At the office today you are likely to find leaders monitoring employee computer use, checking their telephone calls, maintaining checks and balances for certain behaviors, verifying time away from the job and making sure everyone is doing what's expected of them. Some of this is reasonable because employees do abuse their privileges. But in many large corporations the leaders can become timekeepers, "hall monitors". It is difficult for them to motivate their staff when they spend so much time doing activities that put employees on the defensive rather than actions to build their confidence, trust and

loyalty. Positive motivation is more powerful than discipline in changing and affecting behavior.

Treat employees with respect.

Employees are positively motivated by leaders who treat them with respect. A good manager knows their boundaries. They don't say or do inappropriate things. Good leaders know they don't have to be friends with everyone at work but having the respect of others is critical. They listen to their employees, stand up for them and never betray a confidence. Most of all a good manager knows everyone's ego is fragile and it doesn't take much to kill someone's spirit. Correction and criticism is done in a positive way.

Employees are recognized for their accomplishments, thanked for their contributions to the team, praised for meeting their goals, encouraged to grow and motivated to give their best each day.

Negative motivation occurs when leaders do not practice the above behaviors, but typically it goes much further than this. Even with laws against discrimination and harassment, bad leaders often engage in inappropriate management behavior. Employees start to develop negative feelings when mistreated and made to feel they are inferior in some way. Bad leaders don't just point out mistakes but they personally attack their victims. Many times this is done in front of other employees, bystanders, customers and vendors.

Intimidation motivates but are the results really the ones you want....

Leadership by intimidation is a skill many leaders master. Communication centers around if you don't do this you will not have a job. Eventually employees in this type environment internalize the negative messages they constantly hear. They have no job security, their self-confidence is in the toilet, they feel stuck with a boss and in a job they hate. It's extremely difficult for them to muster the motivation needed to work each day.

Motivation is something we all have to work on. Many of us had parents who did not know how to give positive affirmations. We got through childhood somehow but as adults we felt insecure. Eventually you realize you can no longer blame your family or circumstances for your feelings. You seek to know and understand yourself. With that comes self-confidence and acceptance of yourself in spite of all your imperfections. Once you've learned to love yourself you then have something to give others.

Many leaders do not like or love themselves. They put others down and it somehow makes them feel good. Open communication and honesty is discouraged because they feel threatened by those around them. They don't know how to manage so they over-compensate by trying to control everything. They don't feel good about themselves so how can they make others feel good. The incompetent leader feels their own job is threatened. They react by being vindictive and making threats themselves. They are motivating their employees but in a very negative way.

Positive motivation takes personal insight.

Motivating the staff is an inside job first. You can teach bad leaders people skills and how to increase their self-confidence. In today's business environment employees have many uncertainties to deal with. Working for someone who makes you feel good about yourself makes life easier, but if you don't have that it's up to you to motivate yourself. In spite of what others say, know you are special. Don't let anyone else define who you are. If you are mistreated by someone; try not to take it

personally. You choose how to react to all the situations in your life. If you are the leader, do the inner work needed to be positive and motivating to your staff.

> *Motivation is a choice. Even when everything pulls you down make the choice to rise above this.*

Chapter 4

Effective Communicator

A leader can have all the qualities but if they cannot communicate with their followers it's difficult for them to lead.

Communication is not just talking. It is a combination of skills. Effective communicators are good listeners. They pay attention to the details, remember the important things and have the ability to say the right thing at the right time.

Communication from a good leader is positive. They give criticism if needed but don't destroy egos. They use an approach of constructive feedback, coaching skills and combines positive acknowledgement and feedback. Leaders know people react more favorably to praise. They praise more and criticize less. A leader does not reveal everything they know. They don't gossip or engage in communication that's harmful to someone else or to the mission. They limit their complaining to those who can do something about the problem. Conflict is not discouraged but rather controlled so that is productive and useful to the team. A leader knows they will not be friends with everyone but they are friendly. The leader who practices the above principles will have the respect of their staff, customers and vendors.

A small company had a staff team that was dedicated to their work, but challenged by their manager/business owner. His expectations were high but his ability to communicate effectively about expectations low. Instead of clearly communicating what tasks needed to be completed in advance he would outline tasks at the last minute without enough time left to complete the job in a quality way. The staff felt that they had to get the job done, that there wasn't any option. They bent over backwards, worked extra hours, and came in on days off to complete the work. And, despite new tasks being thrown in along the way they completed the work. And as quickly as it was done the next unreasonable task was on the table. There was no acknowledgement that they had gotten an impossible job done, just the high expectation for the next.

What happens to your workforce when you fail to acknowledge or thank them? Workforces decrease performance. Research on worker performance has consistently indicated year after year that money is not the number one motivator for staff, but rather that social praise, success, and acknowledgement rate higher. When business owners and leaders demand, demand, demand and never acknowledge that the staff met deadlines, and that they went above and beyond it becomes demoralizing to staff. Staff becomes frustrated that no matter how hard they work it is never acknowledged. Frustration leads to anger and they wonder why they continue to work so hard.

Simple steps can be taken by managers and owners:

1. Set reasonable goals
2. Agree with staff what is doable
3. Empower staff to plan tasks
4. Acknowledge staff through thank you's and recognition
5. Ask staff for input on systems and operations

Using these simple steps managers can improve the workplace environment and overall work performance. Having a positive, engaged workforce improves the bottom line.

Using an effective employee performance improvement system is another strategy for developing a fully engaged workforce. Staffs that meet with their manager in a positive improvement system are responsive to manager coaching and feedback. When coming out of an environment that has not been positive or acknowledging, managers will need to build trust and rapport.

The employee performance improvement system works with employees to develop a goal plan to improve performance and focus on top goals for the company. Managers shift their management approach to one of Employee Coaching. This shift begins a full company culture shift. A positive engaged employee work culture improves overall business results. The benefits to the organization are tremendous.

The employee performance improvement system involves:

1. Performance improvement planning workshop
2. Manager training in coaching skills
3. Plan review with manager
4. Online tracking of goals and goal progress
5. Monthly coaching with manager, scoring of goals and review of goals.

This results in increased performance productivity and results. It also results in decreased stress around performance appraisals through the monthly coaching process.

Monthly coaching gives managers an opportunity to provide regular feedback, appreciation and acknowledgement. Teams become highly productive and responsive.

Chapter 5

Building a Coaching Environment

Coaching can change the entire workplace.

Coaching is talked about in business, and even on the news. Executives hire coaches, businesses hire coaches and now coach training is brought into many businesses. But why? Why coaching?

Are you a leader, supervisor, manager, business owner that is challenged to work effectively with your staff? If you are like me you were trained to manage people. That's how we were supervised and managed and that's how we manage. It wasn't effective when we were being supervised and it isn't effective, now, as the supervisor.

Why doesn't it work to manage people? People don't want to be "managed", they want to be valued, empowered, inspired, listened to and trusted. To make this shift as a leader many things need to change. Language, labels and behaviors all have to shift. The results that you create by making changes in your approach are worth the work of the change.

Throughout this book you will find new tools, new strategies and in the end you will be equipped to create a new atmosphere in your workplace that is high performing and produces results.

> *As business leaders we want our companies to be vibrant, innovative, creative and have top leaders in our field.*

Organizations often find that they are struggling to achieve this. What happens within the organization that it gets off track or out of alignment? Organizations, like people, have the ability to operate within perfect health, but what the conversation around the coffee pot or the water cooler often is, is about the dysfunction within the organization, the

frustrations of the staff and the negative energy floating and breeding among the organizational community.

Creating work environments that are successful benefits both the employer and the employee. There are tremendous advantages to creating effective workplaces. This book outlines top strategies for realizing an effective team and how you can coach your staff to success, so that they are producing more and better and your business has greater earnings. As the leader, business owner or supervisor your commitment to your staff and their success is an essential key to your overall success. Let's review a few of these essential skills.

Be Real, Be Authentic

In order to build a partnership you must be sincere, real and authentic. If you are not it will be impossible for you to successfully coach staff and build the rapport and loyalty that you want and that your business needs. Staff can read your sincerity. In Employee Coaching, part of the goal is to build a partnership so that staff sees you as the leader/owner/supervisor as an ally, someone that is on their side.

Actually, the goal is to eliminate "sides" and form a working partnership that is aligned around vision, goals and implementation. Your goal as the leader is to have staff fulfilling the company vision and building the results you want.

In fact, there are no sides, only the ones that we create. This approach is about taking down the barriers and the "sides" and working as an effective team. The first step is to remove barriers to communication.

Remove Barriers to Communication

There are many barriers to communication with employees. Some are invisible. They are the barriers that people create in their minds, with their personal history, assumptions and beliefs. These might include

ideas that the boss is unapproachable or a history of working with a boss that was unapproachable.

Our beliefs about the roles each person is in can create barriers to communication. Each individual employee has had different experiences with "the boss" in the past. Most of the time you don't know the employee's past history or experience and how that impacts their current beliefs about you. Their history can linger from school and dealings with authority figures. If they had to go to the Principal's office and it was a negative experience, visiting the Boss' office can bring back that same feeling.

There are also physical barriers to communication.

These can include how the office space is set up. The boss' office can be intimidating in itself. The location of the office can establish "walls". Visiting the office can cause stress for employees especially if "summoned" by the boss. As the supervisor you can work to remove these barriers so that they aren't interfering with your communications.

Some barriers can be easily removed. Move from behind the desk. When you meet with staff sit without desks and tables between you and the employee. You break down barriers to communication and ease the environment for the employee. The desk or table in the middle feels safer. It protects us, but it also changes the communication dynamic. It can set up a power relationship that gives the message of who is the boss and who is the employee. As you work to break down the barriers to communication, rapport and performance this can be an easy one to remove.

If you are meeting with a group of employees, sit in a circle without a large table. Circles are wonderful because everyone can be seen and is equal in the circle. The circle can help remove the "we" vs. "them"

structures that exist. You can work within these circles to establish a safe place for employees to communicate with you. Amazingly, even in a circle, often employees will not sit next to the leader. I have stood in many circles and had a space on either side of me. I call it the "leadership void". But, what it really is, is a fear of filling in that gap.

It is important to note that there will be grumbling when you remove the tables. They provide safety for people and they will use all sorts of excuses why they need them: coffee, notes, books and more. Get past the objections, and observe how the dynamic changes when the barrier is removed. Remember, it will take some time.

Meet outside of your office. Neutral spaces can be good or on the employee's territory is good. The goal is to not meet in a power place. Be present with employees, walk the "floor", know what is happening in their world.

When you meet in a place outside of the "boss'" office you are removing that intimidation. The communication will benefit. Staff will be more empowered to open up communication with you.

Listen To Your Staff

Be open to hearing staff ideas, their observations and let them know what you can and can't do. Staffs have valuable insights and ideas. They are there doing the work of the company or organization. They see what works, what doesn't work and they see why or why not.

This is gold. They have ideas about solutions and improvements. As the owner or supervisor if you are not open to hearing them and using them you won't know about this gold. You will miss it. The company will continue to function in the ineffective or inefficient ways that it has been operating. As the leader, you can create open circles of communication where ideas are valued and welcomed. Share your ideas and ask for their thoughts and feedback. Be willing to be wrong. And

don't just ask for ideas and never use them. If you ask and don't implement anything staff will stop offering ideas because they will feel their ideas aren't valued.

Share Your Vision

It's important to start with vision: the company's and the employee's. What is the company vision? The company vision should be compelling and known by staff. When staff don't know the owner's vision for the company it is hard for them to help move it forward. Having a clear and compelling vision that employees can buy into provides a foundation for success.

Sharing your vision with staff lets them help you in achieving it. Be clear with staff what your vision is for the company. When staff is unclear of the vision of the leaders/owner they cannot be as helpful in accomplishing the vision. They also can't figure out where they fit into the organization, and the direction it is going in. Stating a clear and compelling vision to staff can be inspiring and motivating to staff.

I recommend that you first look at the core purpose of your business, what is the heart of the business? What is the business about, what is at the center of the business? Once you have identified your core purpose you can more clearly outline your vision. What is the direction you are taking the business? Where do you see the business in one year, five years, and ten years? What is the growth, the new products, new services that you want in the business? Are there new buildings or other types of expansion? Is there a business legacy?

Both the core purpose and the vision are important components for staff to know and understand. The core purpose can give staff deeper understanding of your business, the vision gives them an ultimate destination; or at least the destination of where you see taking the company right now.

The core purpose is similar to the mission of the organization but gets even a bit deeper inside the organization and why it exists. The mission gives staff the goal of the organization.

Why Include Staff In The Vision?

Well, if they are working for you but are under an assumption of the purpose of the company and unclear about the direction the company is going; the results can be detrimental to the organization. You want staff working in the direction you are going and not against that direction. Often this can happen as a result of this miscommunication or lack of knowledge and the results have a negative impact on the company. Sharing the company vision can also be an opportunity to gain staff input and ideas for the company. This can be valuable information and make the vision even more compelling. It also brings staff "into the fold"; it lets them know that they are a valued part of the team and company. It is a trust builder.

> *The vision can be exciting, inspiring and ultimately motivating to staff.*

I have met with several leadership teams in which we discussed vision and the vision was unclear to the team. During one meeting the owner of the company talked of his vision, the core of what was important to him in the business. It was different from what the company leaders thought they knew. They were surprised, actually shocked. They gained clarity and understanding of what was important, where their focus needed to be. Vision matters, communicating vision matters more!

But what drives the individual isn't the boss' vision, the company's vision, but their own compelling vision.

Employees can embrace the company vision but...

➡ True success comes from within and from personal vision

➡ Personal vision should be compelling and tie into the company vision

➡ Do you know your employees' dreams and visions for their lives and career?

Find Out About The Staff's Vision

Talking with staff and learning about their vision, their purpose and what they are trying to accomplish is valuable information for you as the leader or owner of the company. Are there ways the organization can support the employee's vision? Does the position that they are in within the organization support their vision as well as the company's? This is the ideal, but sometimes it's not the way that it is.

Looking at how you as the leader can empower the employee to live their vision benefits the company in several ways. It continues to build the relationship between you and the employee, it furthers you as a partner in their success, and when employees see that you are interested in them and their vision, they become more dedicated and motivated to achieve the company's vision, even when they are not there for the long term.

Compelling visions are personal, written in the present tense, in an "as if…" they are happening now, and point to an exciting future. Encourage your staff to write their own compelling vision and share it with you. This type of sharing builds trust and also requires trust. As the supervisor, you hold their vision in confidence as it is theirs to share but you can encourage, and support employees in building their vision. Never ridicule an employee for the vision or use it to tease or embarrass them. This will undermine your goal and ruin your relationship with the employee. It terminates trust, immediately and trust is difficult to repair when it has been severely violated in this way.

Imagine, you have an employee that has always dreamed of going to school. As the leader, you can support this vision. You may have resources that you can access that can directly assist the employee. You may know of resources that could be available for them. You have the ability to flex their schedule. Talking about vision is one of the essential keys to living the vision. When people share their vision with other people, resources, and ideas always appear in some way. It is one way of attracting the vision right to you.

Several times I have encountered leaders that had employees that wanted the boss' job or wanted to open a similar business to theirs. It scared the business leader, but it's really a great opportunity. The opportunity is that the employee has high motivation, high interest in your role, your jobs and tasks. You can use that motivation and interest to train the person, develop the person and at the same time help them in creating their vision. Sure it might be time limited that they are there, working with you, but during that time, they are high energy, highly motivated and that is valuable to you. I have successfully trained subordinates to do my job in several different organizations. The benefit to me was that I could easily be on vacation for long periods of time without concern that the company was suffering. It also facilitated an easy transition when I left the company. There were staff right there ready to step up and fill the vacancy. The downtime for the organization was reduced as well as the cost of hiring a new employee.

Building a coaching environment shifts the entire culture of the organization – the results are positive for the staff and the organization.

Shifting the Workplace to a Coaching Environment

Moving your workplace from a top down management or micromanagement model to one of Employee Coaching for Business Success is an intentional process that requires leadership commitment. For many companies this is a significant change in their management structure and style. There are several steps that managers and leaders should take in order to fully make the transition and have there be a positive performance outcome. You cannot just adopt an Employee Coaching for Business Success Model without doing some planning, preparation and communication about the changes and what they will mean for each staff member. Take the time to move through these steps in order to successfully transition.

First there must be a leadership commitment to the change. Staffs are used to new ideas or consultant teams coming into the workplace and recommending improvements or changes. But they are also used to these changes fading away over time. Their buy in is not 100% because the leadership buy in is not 100%. If, you plan to truly make the shift then there has to be a strong buy in on the part of leaders and a commitment. Without leadership buy in and full on board commitment the coaching approach will not take hold and the organization will be forced to go back to old habits. People's trust in leadership will be reduced and the next new style to come about will be even harder to implement.

If you are the owner of the company, then this means you are the one that has to take on the leadership commitment through your own modeling of implementation and long term commitment to the change.

Employee Coaching for Business Success changes how people are managing and how they are reviewing staff performance. Staffs are more empowered and self-monitoring. The shift can be unsettling for some old time managers. And it can be a bit scary for employees as they become more personally accountable and responsible for their jobs and their performance.

As the leader you must be prepared for the storm, resistance of staff to the changes that you are undertaking. In group dynamics there has been long standing discussion of the stages that groups go through in developing: forming, norming, storming and performing. In adopting an Employee Coaching for Business Success approach, you are in essence saying that you want that performance to improve. It can at first create stress for the team and send them into a resistance stage or storming stage. This is the challenge for the leader to hold fast to their decision and demonstrate their commitment to the plan.

Once you have secured leadership buy in and commitment the next step is to develop your implementation plan. Training staff and managers in the new approach gives everyone the information and shared responsibility for its implementation. You might think that only the leaders and managers need to be trained, but actually the best results will happen when everyone is trained. It makes the environment more collaborative and reinforces the concept of shared responsibility. Imagine, if you just train the managers, which is what typically happens. The program is delivered once again in a top down management style. When everyone is trained then everyone can participate in the implementation phase.

Training includes teaching coaching skills, teaching about how to use the performance appraisal in conjunction with the organizational vision and strategic plan and individual plan goals, and finally on how to provide consistent coaching to staff. Staff learning coaching skills might sound scary to some managers but the reality is that you want the staff on board with a coaching approach. Their understanding of it can help to facilitate that.

Implementation is the exciting part of shifting your work environment because then you start to see changes in the performance environment.

Every staff member should have their new performance appraisal completed. The performance appraisal is at the center of the coaching approach. The performance appraisal tool outlines what's gone well, where the challenges are and the goals for the upcoming year. Those goals should directly tie into the overall strategic plan for the organization. Staff can then see how they fit into the vision of the company and help the company achieve that vision. This is sometimes lost and it is valuable connection for staff.

When the coach and the staff member have agreed upon the goal plan then they can begin the work of accomplishing goals. This is where the real work comes in and the real world coaching. Managers now, have to truly shift from managing and micro-managing to empowering staff to move forward with their goals. When staff buy into their plan and their goals and own them they will work harder to achieve them. The manager or coach's role is to support the staff in implementing tasks that accomplish the goal, identify with the staff member how to achieve the goal and assist the staff member to see how to overcome the challenges that block their success.

This differs from a management style that is telling and directing to one of coaching and collaboration. The coaching approach increases individual staff member's personal responsibility in creating their success and the company's success.

Chapter 6

Coaching Skills

Developing Your Coaching Skills as a Leader & Being Coachable

Already you are developing coaching skills. You are removing barriers to communication, you are being real and authentic and you are building a rapport and partnership with employees. But there are also real coaching skills that are taught in coaching schools around the country and the world. Coaching is a real profession and it has real skills that are part of it. In the resources section I have included the coaching core competencies from the International Coaching Federation (ICF) to further your knowledge of coaching. The skills outlined here are an overview and not a full coach training outline. They will give you a start at learning the needed skills for coaching your staff for success.

The basic coaching skills that you need to employ are:

Be Totally Present

This may be the most important aspect of the coaching relationship. Being Present communicates many things to the staff: interest, honesty, commitment, and value.

For many, this is the hardest and most challenging skill to master. We are so used to multi-tasking that it is difficult to turn it all off and be totally focused and present.

Turn off the email, the phone and close the door to prevent interruptions and distractions. I recently had an employee tell me about their regular meetings with their leader. The leader would move away from them numerous times to check emails and then spend time responding. All the time, saying, go on, go on. This does not build rapport, trust or enhance communication with employees.

Communicate with your team that each employee is valued and that your meeting time with each person is important and should not be interrupted.

Make the time with an employee "their" time; don't multi-task.

Being present means tuning into the person, focusing your energy on them.

Often moving out of your office will also help to facilitate being present as you will not have the distractions that come with your office.

If you cannot be totally present during your coaching meetings with your staff you will find that they are not as effective as they can be.

Listen Deeply With Your Heart

I learned this from a mentor and leader that I worked with. I believe that it says it all in just a few words. When you listen with your heart it is powerful.

When you are totally present you can listen deeply to the other person.

Listen to the person's words and listen to what is not said.

Listen to the whole person, their body language, their words, their facial expressions, their tone, listen to it all.

Maybe you have had training in "active listening" and it is a wonderful skill but here I am talking about listening deeply. It is the act of being fully present and listening with your heart, your wisdom and intuition, as well as your ears and mind.

Ask Meaningful Questions

There are questions that are informational and there are questions that are helpful to the person. In this coaching skill we are asking meaningful

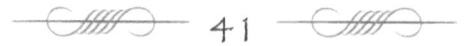

or powerful questions. They help the person to move in new and different directions. They are not just information. That is a different type of question.

Ask powerful questions to help a person move forward.

Questions that challenge the person to grow are powerful and meaningful questions.

Share Observations That Are Helpful

Your observations of an employee can be helpful to them in learning about themselves and achieving their goals.

Share observations in a caring compassionate manner.

This is different from telling employees "you're not doing this right, or that right."

Reframe these observations into a meaningful conversation about performance and how to improve the performance to achieve goals.

Engage and Empower Staff

Engage staff in participating at the highest level possible. Challenging staff through your requests that empower them can also inspire them and give them positive energy.

Empowering staffs asks them to step out of their "comfort zone" or safe space. Whenever you are asking someone to do this it is important to respect where they are. Stepping out of your comfort zone can be a learning experience or it can be a danger experience. Each person has to assess for themselves what that experience is for them

As the coach, you need to be ready to support the person in making new moves.

Coaching is Action Oriented.

It is focused on the present and the future. In Employee Coaching you are working with them to focus on vision and develop a plan of action to move that vision forward. Goal setting is a key component of successfully Employee Coaching.

Action planning is focused on the top goals that the individual is committed to accomplishing.

Coaching comes into play in the review of the performance plan and continuous success focused coaching around the plan.

It is not focused on the past. That is therapy or counseling. Coaches focus solely on the present and the future.

Goal Planning

- Goals tie into the company vision and the employee's vision.

- Goals Point to an exciting future.

- They are positive, specific, measurable, attainable, relevant and time bounded.

- They relate to the company's strategic plan.

- Use the SMART goal formula for each goal.

- Develop goals that are based on the desired outcome or result.

SMART Goals

SMART Goals have certain attributes that make them more effective for tracking and implementation. When you can measure the goal you then know if you are attaining it or making progress. Goals should be results or outcome focused.

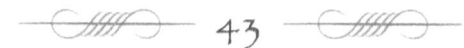

S M A R T

Specific:

* Has clear deliverables or results. When you read the goal you can picture the outcome based on how the goal is written.

Mathematically Measurable:

* Can be counted: How many? How much? Who? There are numbers connected to the goal. When reviewing the goal you are able to see the level of attainment; i.e., 30%, 40% 82% etc.

Attractive and Attainable/Achievable:

* The goal is attractive to you, you want it, and it can be achieved, it's not impossible.

Real, Realistic and Relevant:

* It's a real world goal, realistic and relevant to you, the organization mission and vision.

Think BIGGER and Time-Bounded:

* Think big, stretch yourself and help staff to stretch, but it's a 12 month plan, an annual plan, it is time-bounded. So push the limits but remember the other parts of SMART. But not so BIG that it's impossible.

Goal Examples:

My partner works for a yacht club maintaining a fleet of sailboats. He might have a goal of refurbishing 3 boats this year. At the beginning of his season it feels like a HUGE goal. Three full boats to re-haul. When he breaks the goal down it becomes more manageable.

Perhaps your goal is to increase your income over the next year. A goal such as increase income is just too general. A more specific and measurable goal is:

Increase annual income by 10%.

The goal is specific, measurable – there is a number, there is a time frame, it is relevant to your vision. It meets the SMART goal formula. You can further break the goal down into monthly milestones that are also measurable. Perhaps a 10% increase in revenue means that you have to increase your sales by 10% but it could mean one new program sale per month or one new program sale each week. You have to know your numbers and your business to determine what the specifics are.

When you have the more specific goal of "increasing sales by one per week" then you also know how many more people you need to be in front of to make that happen. Does it take 5 new prospects to secure one new sale or 10 new prospects or 20?

A sales staff might have a sales goal such as increasing personal sales by 20% during the year.

It could be more specific, sales of what, to whom, within what timeframe, but it is generally measurable. Making it "SMARTer" might look like this: Increase sales of solar panels to residential clients by 20% from 100 per year to 120 per year.

Annual goals are typically big. It's important to break them down into smaller steps. Refurbishing three sailboats is big; one boat per month over the course of the winter becomes more manageable. This can be broken down even more for monthly goals that lead to the completion of the annual goal:

Refurbish one boat per month, completing topsides repainted in week one; scrape bottom paint and sand bottom, week 2; clean interior and paint; week 3; paint bottom in week 4.

The sales goal – can also be the foundation for creating a plan to accomplish the goal. How are you going to accomplish it?

- Certain number of cold calls to residents/day.

- A systematic follow-up plan for each lead

- Direct mail, advertising – what are the specifics that are going to create the success?

Breaking goals down can be done in a chronological way. What has to happen first, then what, and on and on. As an educator, we used to break tasks down into all of the little steps that it takes to do the task. Even a task such as tooth brushing can be broken into many steps – 30 or 40 or more. I guarantee that any task you are working on can be broken into steps.

When a goal gets broken down into smaller steps it becomes more manageable and less intimidating. BIG goals can feel overwhelming to a staff member. Helping them to see how it can be accomplished with a task analysis can improve their attitude towards the goal. Tying staff goals into the vision also helps them to see how they fit into the overall success of the organization.

Setting Up Meetings With Employees

Your meetings with employees are invaluable. When you shift your mindset to see them as gold time, truly valuable time that helps the company move the strategic plan and vision forward, it shifts the entire feel of the meeting.

Employees may feel intimidated, especially at first. Remember to:

- Always remove the barriers.

- Don't sit behind your desk.

- Set your intention for the meeting. It's good to think about this in advance and then to share your intention with the employee.

- Ask for the employee's intention.

- Use your coaching skills.

- Be positive

Start the meeting by asking **what is going right for the employee, what's going well?** This gets the employee focused on positive aspects of the job. Even if you are in a meeting to discuss difficult behaviors by starting out in the positive you are shifting the energy. Share your perspective of what's going right. This gives the employee positive feedback from you. And again, the energy is building.

After you have created a positive atmosphere and both acknowledged the positive you can move into the areas that you had called the meeting for. Do this by asking what's not quite right yet? What's not going well? This provides a forum for exploring what is going on. You might find that there are things happening in the work place for this employee that you were unaware of. Perhaps there are other employees that aren't doing what they need to do in order for this employee to complete his/her job. You need to always listen first and not make assumptions about what is going on. In building rapport, your employees are depending upon you to listen to them. This is where your skill of listening deeply, from the heart is vital.

In your discussion with an employee operate from a perspective of personal responsibility. The employee is responsible for their behaviors and actions.

Asking coaching questions gives you the opportunity to explore with the employee what is going on for them especially if their actions are out of alignment with their vision, goals and the company vision and goals.

Building the Staff Up

Just a change from managing or discipline to coaching is going to build people up. But how do we do it even more intentionally? Many staff are walking in your door with a low self-esteem, self-doubts, fears, and self-defeating inner dialogue. We have already talked about listening for the greatness. But now we are going to hear it and help the staff member recognize it for themselves.

Coaches are communicating the client's greatness to them as a part of each session or meeting. It's not flattery, or a search for what can say about their greatness.

In building staff up, we start with a focus on their personal vision, who they are and where they want to go. Work with the staff to identify their values, what's important to them, both in and out of work. List values, just like you did in session one. What are their values? Then focus on the vision, where is it that they are and where do they want to go? As a business owner or the supervisor you might have resources that can help a staff member achieve their vision. What if their vision is to leave? Well, that's ok. They are valuable to you now. You're not wasting time. You are building up a great staff person and supporting them in achieving their vision. Maybe their vision is to finish a degree and get a better position. That's great. You want them to be happy and successful, remember? Write the vision down, in detail, just like you did. Have them include: who, what, where, when, why and how of it.

Once you have clarified the vision you can focus on building them up and supporting the vision, seeing the possibility and their greatness as it relates to it.

Focusing on what is going well, building on successes and how they happen is a shift for many people since we tend to focus on what's missing or what we don't have. In building the staff member up you can start each meeting with them focusing on what is going right?; what are the accomplishments and how did they happen; what makes them right. Get all of that good information about strengths, successes and acknowledge it. If you include the skills the staff member used to accomplish all that they did you begin building a list of skills/tools/strengths that the staff member has. You can also have a staff member recognize their own strengths and attributes, by having them list them, write them down.

Your belief in the staff member and commitment to them as the coach and helping them to win is big factor. So often staff has been alone at the worksite, without the support of a coach that wants them to win. Your belief in them is a simple factor and a critical one. But beyond believing is communicating your belief and commitment to them. Tie it back to their vision and yours. Part of your vision might include the work environment and the type of environment that you envision creating.

If you create an accomplishment list at each meeting and keep adding to the list you have a great resource for affirming the individual's accomplishments and contributions. Work places traditionally lack recognition and affirmation. Often employees don't hear how they are appreciated or that it was observed that they did something that was appreciated. Definitely use your coaching meetings to affirm and recognize accomplishments, but do this between meetings as well. You can send personal notes to an employee or tell them directly, that's even better. A sincere note of recognition and appreciation is remembered and has a positive effect on people. Many workers report never hearing positive feedback from their supervisor or employer. Years and years of research indicate that positive reinforcement especially social

reinforcement increases behavior. So, if you are seeing actions that you like, you want to reinforce them. Telling the person that they did a great job can increase that behavior or action, continuing the great job that they did. If you reinforce someone for solving a problem on their own, then you have just increased that behavior or action and it will happen more and more.

Other ways to build staff up are to: encourage staff. You have talked about vision and next session we are going to talk about goal setting. As the coach you believe in the person and you can encourage them to stretch and reach for their goals and vision. This communicates your support of them and your belief in them and their ability to achieve the desired outcome.

Realize that we are taking coaching skills that people develop through coaching programs over the course of many months or years and filtering it down to two, one hour sessions. There is a lot more that you can learn about coaching. The essence of what I want to convey is that creating a coaching environment within your company or workplace can change the energy and the results that are produced in that work environment. Coaching instead of managing is a great approach to working with people as it values each person and their contribution to the organization.

Chapter 7

Shifting The Manager's Mindset

The annual performance appraisal is an opportunity to enhance employee performance and create greater success for the company and the individual. My intent is to explore how coaching skills can be used in creating a good performance appraisal experience for both the employee and the supervisor and how to keep good performance going throughout the year. As a leader for 18 years my experience was that performance appraisals were a tense time for both the employee and the supervisor. In either position, for me it often felt uncomfortable, so how do we reframe it so that it is a good experience for both?

When managers shift their mindset from a top down performance appraisal to an empowered performance improvement plan the results are solid business results.

Performance appraisals come with a certain mindset. One mindset is of talking about what didn't go well, and where there needs to be improvement. These are sometimes are used as a strategy for firing employees. But what would happen if the mind shift went from telling to collaborating, from planning for success instead of fixing "bad" behavior and one of empowerment and mastery. The performance improvement system does just that. It works to shift the mindset of the manager or supervisor to one of empowering employees to become masters of their results, in charge of their own plan and their success. It also shifts from a "telling" and top down management style to one of coaching and collaboration.

There are several steps to take in making the shift.

One major step is to give up being a controller. To truly empower staff, managers have to let go of being in control of the entire operation. Staff are empowered to set goals, and take action in collaboration with the manager. Now, this doesn't mean that managers are not involved and

can't say no to new ideas. Managers set out their expectations for staff and then staffs establish their plan to meet expectations and exceed them—in essence their performance success plan. Plans are developed in conjunction with the vision and strategy.

Once staffs have established their plan they and their manager review the plan and set milestones, or monthly goals for the plan. When staffs create a well-rounded plan with their manager then managers learn more about the staff, their vision, their personal goals and desires. This information is invaluable to the manager. It allows for more engagement with the employee. It can also provide insights into employee's personal desires that are helpful to the manager in providing needed supports.

Shifting to a coaching framework means several things.

* Meetings occur at least monthly and perhaps more frequently.

* The performance success plan is the center of the meeting. It keeps the plan alive and moving forward and keeps the focus on the top priority goals.

* The manager uses coaching skills to work with the employee.

* Challenges are easily shared because a safe environment has been developed. This allows the employee to share what their challenges are and receive feedback from the manager.

    * Goals are tracked each month. During the meeting there should be a tracking of goals, actually scoring where things are at. This gives you hard core numbers to work with month to month. Both staff and manager can see improvement or problems.

When plans are developed in this way, coaching implemented by managers and goals tracked consistently, the long term results increase. So often during the appraisal goals are set and then never talked about until the following year's appraisal. This is a disservice to employees and

to the company. Employees have no opportunity to share what road blocks or obstacles they are facing. Managers have no opportunity to give feedback, share resources, ideas, or revise goals. These actions are what make goals achievable.

The performance success plan approach makes the annual appraisal a working document that is intentional. Throughout the year the monthly coaching review of the plan and scoring of goals keeps the employee on track and the plan on track. It empowers employees to succeed, and empowers managers to support their staff in success.

Through effective coaching of staff you can further build your business success. Staffs are interested in your success and theirs. By following the steps outlined and developing effective coaching skills you can shift the work culture. As the leader, your skills are paramount in building the business' overall success. People are your business, no matter what business you are in. If you don't treat your people well, you won't be able to build the success you want. Treating people well, recognizing their strengths and tapping into their knowledge and wisdom will only assist you in achieving your vision. As the leader you must be committed to success for the business and for the staff that work in the company.

What does bad or poor leadership cost your company? Well the costs can be unbelievable. There can be costs associated with turnover. Employees are no longer willing to work in bad work environments. The cost of turnover is estimated to be 150% of an entry level person's salary and 200-250% of an executive salary. The national average turnover rate is 25%. What is your turnover rate? Turnover costs take into account replacement of staff, hiring costs, retraining costs and loss of work performed during this period of time.

Do the calculation using an entry level salary at $25,000. One hundred and fifty percent of that is $37,750. That is your cost losing one employee due to poor leadership. What if you were to lose ten? That's $350,000 that you just lost.

But turnover is not your only cost. What if poor leadership leads to poor communication and that leads to material losses as a result. Can you afford to waste materials? Perhaps your company has a material loss of $1000-$2000 per contract. Is that loss built into the contract pricing? How are you able to justify the loss? Do you ever see waste because one department or area of your company fails to communicate effectively with another? This often happens within organizations when staffs become territorial or operate within their own departmental silos.

Communication fails and staff are only focused on their area of the company instead of seeing the bigger picture. They instead want to lay blame on other departments for the failure instead of taking responsibility and accountability for their role in the overall success of the organization.

Leadership development can be a successful strategy for improving communication, leadership function and overall organizational accountability.

By taking on leadership as a real world skill that needs to be developed, organizations achieve new levels of success. When teams, leaders and staff are all on the same page, working on the same vision, the same strategic plan and know HOW to communicate they are able to work effectively, often achieving more than they even imagined.

> *Effective and Pro-Active Communication can save you many hours of downtime, and hassle*

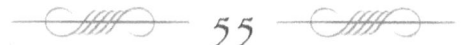

Chapter 8

Enhancing the Performance Appraisal Process

Moving into a positive performance appraisal framework...

Our Current Appraisal Framework

Often, during the performance appraisal, the manager talks about issues that the employee didn't know were coming. Today we are talking about how to reframe the experience for both the employee and the manager. With the manager as a coach and partner committed to the employee's success the environment can shift. The goal is to reframe the experience, creating a positive, goal oriented environment that thrives on success and enhancing performance. In working with many groups of people solving problems, when they focused on what was going well and built upon it they were more successful than when they worked on what the problems were that they were having and what they needed to improve. In focusing on solutions, they ultimately identified the things that needed improvement as well.

It's important to recognize your feelings about performance appraisals and to imagine the employee's perspective.

* History of being an uncomfortable experience

* Reframe the experience & create a positive, goal oriented environment that thrives on success, enhancing performance

* An opportunity to tune into the person and find out what is going on with them

* Create a plan for the upcoming year

* Most individuals (most employees) want to be successful

Start With Vision

It's important to start with vision: the company's and the employee's. What is the company vision? The company vision should be compelling and known by staff. When staff don't know the owner's vision for the company it is hard for them to help move it forward. Having a clear and compelling vision that employees can buy into provides a foundation for success.

But what drives the individual isn't the boss's vision, the company's vision, but their own compelling vision.

* Employees can embrace the company vision but…

* True success comes from within and from personal vision

* Personal vision should be compelling and tie into the company vision

* Do you know your employees dreams and visions for their lives and career?

Take Time To Create A Vision

If the employee hasn't thought about their vision, take the time to create a vision with them. Does their vision, their passion tie into the company vision? Can you as the supervisor help the employee to achieve their vision? What if their vision is your job? Well, that's great. As supervisors, managers and leaders part of our role is mentoring and developing our employees. It's great to have employees that are motivated to learn and grow. It's also great to have employees that know your job and can do it competently.

Compelling visions are personal, written in the present tense, as if…they are happening now, and point to an exciting future. Encourage your staff to write their own compelling vision and share it with you.

Use Coaching Skills To Develop Success and Excellence

Where are we at now? After you have created a compelling vision, find out where we are at right now. By using six key coaching questions you can quickly get to where the employee is at. In these questions you have the opportunity to create powerful positive energy, find out what the gaps are and what the resources needed are. In talking about what would be ideal you are also focusing a bit back on the vision, but you are also pointing in the direction that you need to go– so how do we get there?

When meeting with a staff member

* Be present

* Tune into them and tune out everything else

* See their greatness

Use Six Coaching Questions:

These basic six coaching questions create a positive framework that gives you the ability to set a solution focused environment that is empowering and positive. You as the supervisor or manager, still have the space to deal with challenges and difficult behavior.

1. What's going right?

2. What makes it right?

3. What is it that would be ideal?

4. What's not quite right yet?

5. What would make it right?

6. What resources do you need?

(Based on the Six Question Process developed by Dr. Marshall Goldsmith: http://www.marshallgoldsmithlibrary.com)

As the supervisor, I see my role as one of supporting my staff so that they can do their job. I'm their coach, their success partner and the person that is helping to get them the resources they need to do their job. As the director of an outdoor center, my job was to get the clients there, but it was also to make sure that our resources were there for the client, and that we had the infrastructure we needed to provide the service– the ropes course, trained staff, food for meals.....

Create a Plan For Excellent Performance

Work with each staff person to create a goal plan. This creates a positive framework to operate from and is positive focused instead of problem focused. Identify the different roles they have in their life and at work so that you can create a comprehensive plan. Keep it simple with at most 10 goals. Including personal goals helps to remind both you and the employee that there should be life/work balance. Start with what is going well and create goals that build on those successes. Write goals that are SMART: specific; measurable; achievable; relevant; time bound.

You, the supervisor become the partner or the coach – coaching for success. In creating a plan focused on success for the employee, the manager begins to shift the paradigm to one of employee and coach/partner. As supervisors, our role is build successful teams and we have to have successful team members in order to do that. If we focus on creating success we are more likely to create it. Focus on the positive, the solutions. What's going right, how do we create more of it? In working with teams I have found that when I focus on what they are doing well and how we do more of it – we build on our success.

When we create goals that are SMART, we can measure them, and track their progress. If goals are soft, not measurable, it becomes difficult to progress the plan or give any feedback. So, how do we make them measurable? Measurable is countable, how many, when, who?

Let's review the SMART goal format again:

SMART Goals

SMART Goals have certain attributes that make them measurable. When you can measure the goal you then know if you are attaining it. Goals should be results or outcome oriented and not focused on the process.

Specific:

Write the goal with a specific outcome or result.

Measurable:

Can be counted: How many? How much? Who?

Attractive and Attainable:

Is reasonably attainable, can be achieved within reason, a stretch but not so far out it is impossible.

Relevant:

Goals are relevant to the person's position, the organization, the vision, values of the company.

Think Bigger and Time-Bounded:

Write goals for the appraisal that can be accomplished within the timeframe of a year.

This is an opportunity to reframe the experience and create an annual plan that is positive, focused on the future and compelling. The annual performance appraisal is an opportunity to enhance employee performance and create greater success for the company and the individual.

Once you have set goals your partnership has begun. Part of what makes the performance appraisal uncomfortable is that for many it is the only time of the year that their performance is discussed so openly. This plan becomes the center of your partnership with the employee. The plan needs to be kept alive and in front of you both. You have focused during this meeting on what has gone well and how you can build upon that over the next year. It is important to keep the goals alive during the year and not wait until the next appraisal to discuss them again. This just keeps the old framework of stress and discomfort going. The first step in keeping it alive is to...

Break Goals into Achievable Steps

Often goals feel big and that "bigness" makes them overwhelming. Break goals down into the small actions that are needed to accomplish the goal. Identify which step you will take first. Steps can be smaller goals that the employee works on each month. Select doable steps and write them down.

There are a couple of ways to do this. One is to take a goal and break it down into all the steps it will take to accomplish it. I put it on a chart that I can then refer back to. Each week or month you work on one of the steps or a part of a step. Typically, each step can be broken down into more steps. You and the staff person have to decide how many steps work for you. It should be clear and easy to understand.

Build in Accountability

Building in accountability in your annual success plans is the key to success. How many performance appraisals have you had or have you done, that didn't get looked at until the next year?

You need to meet with people regularly and review the goals. It's unfair to come at a staff person at the end of the year and say you didn't accomplish what we outlined in your plan. Yes, you can accomplish

some things just by writing down the goal, but the level of accomplishment is usually lower than what we want in our companies.

The key to success is building in accountability through regular meetings, weekly, bi-weekly or at minimum, monthly. We often fall short on keeping a plan alive because we aren't having regular meetings that review the plan. Regular meetings keep focus on the plan and keep it moving forward.

Meeting with employees on a regular basis provides a framework for talking about goals, scoring goals and figuring out what happened and what the next steps are. This is your **partnership meeting**. It should occur at least monthly. This gives employees feedback and a chance to talk with you about the challenges they are facing and how to overcome them. If the employee feels that you are on their side, they will risk being honest with you.

Regular check-ins help keep people focused. When people know they have set out to accomplish a task by a certain date or the next meeting they are more likely to do it. When there is an accountability structure employee's know that it's important, it matters and they're going to be asked about it. When you set goals and then never check back in on the progress, employees can interpret that the goals didn't really matter and aren't important to you.

Celebrate success, write down accomplishments, and build on success. Celebrate with employees their success. Most supervisors fail at recognition and acknowledgement. For some reason, we are uncomfortable saying "good job". But when we celebrate success we increase success. It is basic behavior intervention: reinforcement increases behavior. If the only time a person receives attention is when negative things happen, those negative things they are being reinforced as well. We, as supervisors, could be increasing negative behavior unintentionally. Taking a positive celebration approach to accomplishments is a more productive strategy. Positive celebrations

build positive energy and most people will increase their positive and productive behavior. This is our goal as the supervisor or manager. So use positive celebrations, recognition and acknowledgement as a strategy for increasing success within your organization.

Monthly Accountability

Meet with staff at least monthly and review the plan. Bringing out the plan and talking about it, keeps it alive. If it is never mentioned it gives staff the impression that it wasn't that important and they don't need to work on the goals outlined. Remember the goals outlined are focused on creating better results for the company. You want that. Focus on the plan. At the monthly meeting spend time to:

- Review the vision

- Review the accomplishments (What's going right?)

- Review the goals

- Score each goal – give it a percentage 60%; 85%

- When a goal is falling short use coaching skills to help figure out what the problem is and how to change it.

- Does the leadership need to shift to provide more supervision, training, direction....?

You are looking for success of at least 80%. If the person is in their own way, do they need to make a shift in their feelings, beliefs, paradigm, to move forward and get themselves out of the way? Are they choosing not to make the necessary shift. It's an opportunity to talk about choices that we make. We each operate from a place of personal responsibility. We are responsible for ourselves, our actions. If there are company

barriers, it is the time to figure out what they are and how to eliminate them.

> *Measurable goals can be scored.*
> *Score the goals each month.*

When you actually score goals you are able to see progress or regression from month to month. You are also establishing a concrete way of looking at the goals. It is not a feeling that something is better or worse, you are able to see it clearly because you have created goals that are countable.

If the goal is below 80% talk about what's in the way? Is the individual in their own way?

Go back to the six coaching questions (Remember? Here they are again!):

1. What's going right?

2. What makes it right?

3. What is it that would be ideal?

4. What's not quite right yet?

5. What would make it right?

6. What resources do you need?

Create a Partnership

The monthly review of the PLAN gives you the opportunity to really check-in with staff and support them in developing success. It also prevents the annual performance review dread. They know you are invested in their success as well as that of the company. This is powerful.

It develops you as a leader and partner of the staff member and lets you know where the focus needs to be. It also creates a regular stream of communication-both ways that can only improve results.

These partnership meetings must be prioritized by you, the leader. Don't schedule them and then reschedule them and continue putting them off. They are one of the keys in your plan for Employee Coaching to success.

Now, let's be clear, coaching is not built solely on six questions. There is much more to what a coach learns and trains on. But in this framework, it is a simplified way of shifting from a managing approach to a more coaching approach, combined with the other skills: of being present, listening deeply, removing barriers to communication, accountability etc. Coaching enhances the workplace and the overall success of the organization.

Certainly additional skills in coaching can be developed for managers through effective coach training for manager programs. This handbook is designed to get you thinking and started in a new approach. It is a beginning for shifting your work environment.

Handling Poor Performance

I believe that coaching skills can help you as a supervisor create better success. When there is poor performance the coaching questions give you an opportunity to build success, as you have also built a framework for having real conversations. We are all adults, and we each have personal responsibility and make choices about our behavior. If you do use discipline or progressive discipline in your organization, you need to have a clear policy on it and employees need to be informed of the policy. They also need to know the expectations and job responsibilities of their position. With that foundation you can have real conversations about their behavior and choices and the position it puts you in. In this

approach, your behavior as a supervisor should be a consequence of the employee's behavior. Discipline is not handed out randomly or lightly.

In a coaching environment it remains important that employees are "called" on inappropriate behaviors. Tardiness, not showing up for work, not following through on work task assignments each require the supervisor and coach to follow up with the employee. It is an opportunity still to improve performance.

Failing to confront an employee that does not show up for work or does not do their job up to par empowers the employee to continue to do just that. Changing behavior takes the courage of the supervisor to talk with the employee and challenge the employee to take responsibility for their action and figure out solutions to change the behavior.

These are the conversations that many supervisors find are uncomfortable and difficult. When a coaching environment has been created that includes regular accountability meetings as outlined, these conversations become easier. There is rapport and shared vision, strategies and goals.

I understand the hesitancy and it takes to time to reframe the work environment. But clear communication is vital even when it is hard. I've had this conversation with staff in a union shop, in a supervisory session that involved poor performance.

And in having these conversations – it's important to remember that our goal is success and the employee's goal is to be successful also. Employee retention is important to everyone.

Employee Retention is Two-Sided

- Employer Perspective

    o High cost to fire staff

    o High costs to replace employees

- o High costs to recruit and train employees

- o Time – a lot of time to recruit, hire and train

* Employee Perspective

- o Risk in finding another job

- o Loss of income/benefits

- o Negative impact on personal life, family

It can feel so much easier to quit a difficult job or fire a challenging employee but the impact on both is huge. As the manager or leader, if there is a way to coach an employee to succeed it is definitely preferable. When you look at the actual costs of hiring, retraining, lost work time, shuffling other staff around to cover, it is a lot of money. It may at first appear easier but there is a big cost to the organization in time and resource, as well as to you the manager. You will be the one putting all of the time into find the new person, train the new staff (from scratch) and keep things running smoothly in the meantime.

Go back to the coaching questions – it gets them talking about what is going right, what their vision for success is and what is in their way.

Help staff to identify how they limit themselves. The beliefs they have that get in their way, the old messages they have been told or told to themselves that place limits.

To create the success you want: Keep focused on your goals.

Staying focused on your goals and those of your employees keeps the momentum going. As the supervisor you can create a positive and encouraging environment and create a performance culture.

Chapter 9

Implementing a Performance Improvement System

As we have discussed, performance appraisals are often a stressor for managers and employees alike. They are put off, ignored and each party hopes they will just go away. But the performance appraisal does not have to be a negative event; in changing the framework of the appraisal it can be a positive experience for both and provide positive outcomes for the company.

How do you do your performance reviews? Do you stress for weeks ahead of time, avoid, procrastinate and just put it off? Some companies don't even use them at all, failing to see their value in performance improvement, while other companies do them but with negative impacts on their employees.

For many companies performance appraisals are the tool that they use to fire or terminate employees. But, with the rising cost of turnover to the company you really CANNOT afford to fire people that you have invested in. Of course, sometimes that is the only option, but often it is not the best option because the employee can participate in an effective performance improvement program and become one of your BEST employees.

Performance appraisals are usually the leader or manager telling an employee what they did well and what they didn't do well. The employee dreads this as does the manager. Telling people that they are not doing well in their job is hard work and uncomfortable for all.

It is time to change your paradigm about the performance appraisal and perhaps even shift how and why you do them. What if you took that appraisal and instead of it being the once a year time when you delivered bad news you shifted it to be a positive plan for performance improvement? What do you think would happen to employees; to your company productivity and results? And how would the manager's experience change? Perhaps they would focus more on the performance improvement plan.

The Performance Improvement Paradigm suggests that you shift performance appraisals to Performance Success Plans. There is still room for feedback and room to improve in areas where there needs to be improvement. The big paradigm shift is in the approach. The Performance Improvement System takes you to a positive planning process, teaches coaching skills to both managers and staff. Goals are tracked throughout the year. Through monthly Gold Time meetings employees are able to discuss with their "coach" and manager what is going well, what is still not going well and the road blocks to success. When managers learn to coach staff through the barriers and road blocks then performance can continue to shift and improve.

The Performance Success Plan can be conducted in employee groups with an outside facilitator that takes the burden off of managers and leaders when using our highly recommended Best Year Yet™ system. The manager's role then becomes one of providing input and focus but the employee and facilitator create the actual plan. Employees need to take personal responsibility in creating an honest review and plan. Managers need to shift their role to one of telling employees bad news to coaching them to succeed.

By teaching coaching skills to managers, employees begin to benefit from a positive coaching approach. Coaching skills and performance tracking give the manager tools that they can use to help employees to stay on track. By shifting to a positive framework, employees see that the company is interested in them beyond their work performance because the planning can also include their personal goals. As a manager, when you know your employees personal and career goals, you are in a position to support them in their goals. This positive strategy results in better work performance, increased company loyalty and consequently overall company results improve.

The performance improvement system is implemented in conjunction with the overall company vision and strategic plan. It brings the entire company into the fold of working in a focused and performance based way. Tracking goals and providing regular feedback and coaching accelerates results for individuals, teams and the company. Having employee Performance Success Plans that each tie to the overall strategy of the company; increases the results that the company can achieve. No longer are employees working on non-essential tasks that don't better the company's vision.

By shifting to a positive performance improvement focused appraisal and success plan instead of a punitive appraisal system shifts the entire outlook of the team and workforce. Positive outcomes are numerous and turnover costs reduced. So in addition to increased performance results the company saves money in turnover, retraining, rehiring etc. The company has created a positive energy that runs throughout the entire workforce. The shift is vibrating results throughout and the overall company vision comes to life for the entire company instead of just the leaders.

Chapter 10

Real Conversations

Have Real Conversations With Your Staff

Real conversations are honest, straight forward, to the point and non-judgmental. The conversation isn't about accusing or blaming but letting a staff member know what is happening.

An example of a real conversation was one that happened for me years ago. I was the manager, meeting with a staff member for a disciplinary meeting. The staff member had opted to not have his union rep present. He worked a night shift and was a long term employee with many good qualities. I liked him. I liked his energy in his work. But he had had many disciplinary issues. We were meeting because he had failed to show up for work for the third time. We had had meetings prior to this one. Our disciplinary policy was progressive. He had received a verbal warning and written warning both directing him that he needed to report for work when scheduled and that he needed to call a supervisor if he wasn't going to be at work so that a replacement could be scheduled. The meeting we were in was for further disciplinary action: a 3 day suspension. The conversation acknowledged the value he gave to the organization. It all went something like this:

Supervisor: *Hi _____. I think you know why we are here today. We had another incident of not showing up for work and not calling in to let the staff and the supervisor know you wouldn't be in. Is this correct?*

Employee: *Yes.*

Supervisor: *First, I want to say that I really enjoy having you on the team. You have so many wonderful skills and talents that I really value. You are liked by the clients; you are creative in your interactions with them; and bring your creativity to work with you. But those strengths aren't helpful to us when you don't show up for work.*

Employee: *I know.*

Supervisor: *When you don't show up for work it puts the site into a really difficult position. Typically, someone needs to stay on site and work a double shift. I know that this has happened to you and you understand how frustrating it could be to have to work a double shift. In our past conversations I have had the impression that you liked your job. What is it about your job that you like?*

Employee: *Well, there is quite a bit that I do like….*

Supervisor: *That is great. I am glad to hear that you still like your job, because you do bring real strengths to the team. Tell me what is going on in your life right now that is interfering with you getting to work.*

Employee: *I am having some things going on right now.*

Supervisor: *Let's talk a bit more about what's happening and see if we can come up with some solutions.*

Employee: *Shares more details about the challenges they are facing personally.*

Supervisor: *Ok, so what can we do to change this, so it's not happening? Right now, I'm in a position that I have to take action. You know that. I can't ignore your actions. But my main interest is in helping you to find ways to be here successfully.*

Employee: *I know.*

Supervisor: *My preference is to be supportive to you, to have meetings with you about all the things that are going well; to spend our time creating greater success and to help you find solutions to the challenges you face both here at work and in your personal life.*

Employee: *I understand that you have to take action. I'm sorry.*

Supervisor: *OK Right now you and I both know that I have to take action and that because this has happened several times in the past and we have multiple conversations about not showing up for work, I have to suspend you from work for three days.*

Employee: *I know.*

Supervisor: *Let's talk a minute about the things you could do over the next three days that will help you to resolve your conflict and enable you to be at work. Do you have any ideas for actions over the next three days?*

Employee: *Yes, I can.... And I need to....*

Supervisor: *Those sound like some great ideas.*

Employee: *Thanks.*

Supervisor: *Do you understand that you could be fired for this, if you and I don't figure out some solutions?*

Employee: *Yes*

Supervisor: *I want to avoid that. I value having you on the team, but I also need someone that is reliable on the night shift. I would like you to be proactive and give me a call if you see something coming down the road that is going to be a problem for you. Maybe together we can figure out some solutions so it doesn't end up back here again. Is that something you can do?*

Employee: *Yes.*

Supervisor: *Now. You __are__ suspended for three days but when you come back, I want you to check in quickly with me and let me know if you were able to accomplish anything.*

Employee: *Ok, I will. Thank you. I will see you on....*

The discussion was respectful and the employee took personal responsibility for his actions. He understood his actions put me, as the supervisor, in a position where action had to be taken. We had had similar conversations in the past. Personal responsibility is important for each member of a team to understand. Each employee needs to understand that they are personally responsible for their behaviors and

actions, and that their actions or behaviors dictate consequences. When the employee does xyz behavior then this consequence occurs. This is outlined in employee handbooks and company policy. As the manager and coach you can remind the person of their personal responsibility in creating the situation. They may put the supervisor in a position of discipline. That is what this conversation was about, reminding the employee of their role.

The conversation was "real" because we were each talking from our truth. Sharing our observations and what we each saw as the story.

Real conversations are honest. It was also "real" because it wasn't offensive, authoritative or demeaning. It acknowledged him and his value to the team and it acknowledged the needs of the organization. It laid it all out for him.

Even with a coaching approach to management and supervision there are times when employee behavior requires intervention. Using a coaching approach when this happens is still more respectful and productive than an authoritative approach. It is a blending of coaching and progressive discipline. As a manager, there are work expectations. Coaching does not mean that employees can take advantage of the employer and not have to show up, do their job, etc. It means that a working relationship is built that is more effective. With a good rapport established between the supervisor and employee these types of behaviors are reduced.

> *Being real, direct and authentic in your communication with staff facilitates more effective communication and greater rapport.*

Chapter 11

Screaming Employees?

How to effectively resolve conflicts in the workplace

Do you have employees that are out and out fighting with each other at work? Yelling, screaming, not getting along or perhaps has difficult relationships with their supervisor?

Conflicts in the workplace happen frequently and the fallout can be costly to the employer and the employee. Developing the skills to resolve conflicts that arise can save your company significant money. First let's look at the costs:

* Decreased productivity due to the emotions involved in interpersonal conflict

* Time lost from work by employees

* Time lost from work by managers involved in the conflict

* Recruitment and training of new employees

* Decreased productivity by other staff due to tension/stress and the overall work environment

The root of many conflicts is communication: either unclear communication, resulting in misunderstandings or lack of communication; or harsh communication that gets blocked out. One strategy to address rising incidents of conflict is communication training. Teaching people how to listen and how to talk clearly can prevent and decrease conflicts.

Communication is such a challenge. So often, we feel we have been really clear, only to find out that the other person really misunderstood us. Being a clear communicator takes commitment. You need to be able to talk in a neutral tone, eliminating inflammatory emotions. Speak from the heart and listen from the heart are good basic guidelines. Beyond the basics are to: listen deeply to what the other person is saying and then check-in with them. Ask them: "is this what you are saying?" It lets the person you are talking with know what you have understood and gives them the opportunity to clarify or correct misunderstandings.

Conflict resolutions is the perfect place to use coaching skills and real conversations.

What do you do when the conflicts have escalated? Resolving conflicts are good for everyone involved, but sometimes, in the moment, it's hard for the people directly in conflict to see that. As mentioned earlier, conflict is costly. As the owner, or manager we forget that there is a great cost, not only to us, but also to the employee. Changing jobs due to a conflict means a great deal of change for an employee. They might not be able to get the same level of pay; benefits; shifts, etc. that they are accustomed to. The impact to the employee and their family can be high.

As the leader you can setup an effective environment to resolve the dispute by following some simple steps and laying out a couple of guidelines.

First, spend time talking with each person involved. Let them know that your belief is that developing a shared solution is important to each person and that you value each of the employees involved. During the individual meetings you can begin to gather information about what they see as the possible solutions. Let the employees know that your intent is to meet with each of them and then with them together, to talk about their perspectives and possible solutions to the conflict.

During these individual meetings use the six basic coaching questions:

1. What's going right?

2. What makes it right?

3. What would be ideal?

4. What's not quite right yet?

5. What could make it right?

6. What resources do you need?

Remember, we start in the positive. It brings in some positive light to a challenging situation. You might have to push the individual to reflect on the positive. Don't negate or leave out the "what's not right, yet?" question. This gets you into the "muck". By following up with "what would make it right?" you start to shift the conversation to solution focused. In the midst of anger and conflict you might have to get past some unreasonable solution suggestions, but encourage each person to brainstorm some ideas. Let them know how the meeting with the other person will be set up and that in that meeting you will all be brainstorming solutions.

Use a simple & effective process:

Create a safe space for involved parties to talk. (Private, neutral)

Set out the guidelines:

- Only one person talks at a time

- No interruptions, defending or justifying

- Come in with an open mind, open to the possible solutions and be willing to compromise.

Give each person an opportunity to tell their story, from their perspective. Remind the other people involved that we are each

listening, listening to each person's perspective. This is a key. There are always three stories: my story; your story and THE story; or your truth; my truth and THE truth. What really happened usually lies somewhere in the middle of each story, as we each tell stories from our own perspective, history and interest?

Paraphrase the stories of each person. This ensures that each story has been understood. Using phrases such as "What I am hearing you say is…. Is that right?" Sometimes this is called "reflecting back." Essentially you are taking the person's statement and rewording it back to them and checking if you have understood it.

After everyone has had an opportunity to tell their story, **brainstorm possible solutions.** Again, this isn't a time to judge. Whenever you are brainstorming you want all the ideas, good or bad, or out in left field. One of them might be the idea that helps someone come up with the BEST solution.

Identify the solutions that work for each party. It is important that the solution is agreeable to each party and the company. In order for the agreed upon solution to work and be successful, you need buy in from all parties.

Agree to do the solution. The last step is the key to moving forward. You are seeking agreement from everyone on the solution. If there is no agreement, then as the owner or leader you have the option to make the decision. Informing people that without their agreement, you will decide and everyone will have to live with that decision. It is yours to make if necessary.

Some common pitfalls:

- Don't take sides. As the manager your interest is the company, the resolution of the conflict and each employee.

- Don't mandate a solution; you want the staff invested in the solution.

- Don't select the solution unless it is absolutely necessary.

What do you do if staff members refuse to participate in conflict resolution?

Offering staffs the opportunity to resolve conflict is a much better option than being disciplined, having supervisor mandated solutions or taking no action at all. When staffs refuse to cooperate or participate, it's time to talk with them about your company policies, their personal responsibility for their behavior and actions and your responsibility as the owner or manager to take actions based on their behavior. The intent of this type of conversation isn't to threaten disciplinary action, but to talk about the reality of the situation and the need to resolve it.

Each individual makes choices, as supervisors our actions are based upon the behaviors and actions of the employee. As the supervisor you are encouraging good choice making, but the reality is that some people will make a poor choice and choose to continue to act in ways that are not acceptable in your workplace. In these situations you must then follow your organization's disciplinary policies as outlined for your employees in the employee handbook. Resolving the conflict and creating a good work environment for everyone is my first choice as the manager/supervisor/owner.

Conflicts in the workplace can be successfully resolved, by listening. Giving each person space to tell their story validates them and communicates to them their value to you and the organization. Using the simple process outlined keeps you moving in a positive direction.

Chapter 12

The Bully In The Manager's Office

Bullies don't just exist on the playground. They also sit in the manager's chair or the CEO's office.

Bully leadership is sharp, authoritative, angry, and feels uncomfortable to those in contact with it. Bully leaders believe that they are rallying the troops, getting everyone on board. But that is not what happens. The bully leader barks out orders, threatens consequences and uses strong, harsh statements to "motivate" people to do what the leader wants.

The "motivation" that results is limited. And that is what the "Bully Leader" doesn't realize. Bully Leaders are scary for people so they do what they need to do but there is a sacrifice. The sacrifice occurs in the work performed. People do what needs to be done and that is all. They don't go above and beyond. They don't share their knowledge and ideas with the leader. The Bully Leader wants and needs to be the one with the great ideas. They don't want to share the limelight.

The bully leader believes their approach is working because they see results. They don't see the limitation or the impact of their style. What they see are results. The results are what needed to occur. The Bully Leadership style is reinforced and continues on. What they fail to see is the results that could have happened with a more open, empowering leadership style. They fail to see the impact of their leadership on their staff. They fail to recognize the negative effects. These negative impacts are costly to the company. As a result:

People are not empowered.

Bully Leaders Miss Out On The Great Ideas Of Their Staff.

* People respond with decreased motivation, interest and commitment or loyalty. This can lead to decreased productivity and quality.
* People may have physical responses that increase absenteeism.
* People may have their emotional responses that mirror the leaders creating a bullying atmosphere that permeates the organization.

What Motivates The Bully Leader?

Bully Leaders want control. They lack trust in other people. They believe that no one will or can do the job as well as them. Out of their fear and lack of trust comes their assertion of aggressive behaviors. They also have a history of using bullying techniques to control their world. It has a history of working for them, feeling empowering to them and maintaining their own safety.

The results of the bully leader are far less than that of an empowering coaching leader. This effective leader trusts that people can and will do their job. Through their empowerment, staffs exceed expectations. The leader has time to create new business opportunities, nurture existing client relationships and pursue greater results.

A bully leader can shift and become a empowering coaching leader through intentional focus and work. There are several steps they need to take to make this shift:

* Recognize that their bullying approach is not effective
* Commit to the change
* Work with a coach to learn: coaching skills, creating a coaching work environment and empowerment strategies
* Work with the team to transition from being bullied to being coached. This step is the hardest because it requires trust on both sides and trust has not existed for this team in the past. The leader will have to build trust and be patient during this

transitional time. Their commitment to change will have to extraordinary to demonstrate their trust of others and their willingness to risk their own vulnerability.

* Recognize accomplishments of the team and each success.

Bullying behavior can be shifted to that of a collaborative leader with focused work on the part of the leaders. Organizations continue to recognize the negative impact a bully has their overall outcomes and work to shift the leader's behavior or move bullies out of the organization. Take action today to shift your organization to one of empowerment and collaboration and see the results within the company change. The benefits are astounding. You will see increases in employee performance, loyalty, idea generation and sharing, team work, focus, and implementation of strategic goals. These all contribute to improved overall success of the organization.

Chapter 13

Working Effectively with Your Team

Building High Performing Teams Produces Powerful Bottom Line Results

Creating a powerful work place that is focused and intent on success is one of the biggest challenges business owners face. What is a powerful workplace? Powerful workplaces are focused, strategic, and intentional. Owners and staff are action oriented in ways that move the business. They do not waste time on activities that are not focused on the success of the company.

Well, how do you do that? First, is to create an intentional strategic plan that is focused on your company's success in all areas. It is important to include the entire team in the planning session. Take time to hear what is working well, and celebrate it. Then spend time, hearing what isn't working so well. It is important to be open to this step. This isn't a time to dwell on what's not right, just to get it out there. There is vital information in both what works well and what doesn't work well. That vital information is the wisdom of those closer to the day to day workings of the company. Is it possible that the greatest solutions could come from unexpected places? **Most definitely!** Staffs on the front line see both the problem and have ideas about the solutions.

After you have gathered this vital information look at what gets in the way of the team's success or the company's success. Often we have created our own road blocks. Sometimes they are in terms of systems (that we created), often they are rules (that, we also created), and sometimes it is in how we think individually or as a team. This is a hard step, because it takes deep thinking and honest reflection. Teams can be scared of doing this work, but it is very important to moving the company forward.

Once you have identified how the team is in "their own way" of success you can create a new attitude or approach to success. We recommend doing this in a positive statement that points to an exciting future.

Now, you are ready to develop the strategies for moving there. Write your strategies in the form of measurable goals. Things you can really count, so that you can track your success. A goal such as "improving the company" is too vague. Instead write, "increase revenue by 25%". That is measurable. Limit your strategic goals to ten. This enables you and your team to stay very focused. If they come up with 100 find the top ten.

After goals are established you begin working with intention. Each day staff and leaders should be working to achieve the strategic plan. If your operations involve tasks that aren't focused on these strategies evaluate whether outsourcing these tasks would improve your results with the increased time to focus on implementation. Or are there other ways you improve the focus of the team?

Maintain implementation. After a strategy session, everyone is often excited and enthusiastic, but quickly the day to day operations interrupt your focus. Schedule, at least monthly strategy review meetings. Don't bring other agenda items to the meeting. These meetings are solely for reporting on the strategies and scoring them. Each person that has taken responsibility for a strategic objective comes to the meeting prepared to report on the results that have occurred. This reporting is in terms of numbers. The strategy was achieved at ___%, giving you a clear picture of where you are. This group accountability is powerful. It creates a culture of performance, a focus on success and achievement. The Performance Success Plans can then be coordinated with the company's vision and strategy. The individual Performance Success Plans already are helping individual team members to be results focused.

Effective teams are meeting at least monthly to review goals. They have closed the gap in performance and communication to enable greater results.

When teams are each working on their personal strategies for success and come together and work on team strategies together, then score their goals, communicate about successes and challenges the performance culture shifts to one that is focused on goals, top strategies and accomplishing the company vision.

Team building around the strategic plan is a powerful process of collaboration and ongoing implementation and accountability. Teams that stay focused on the plan produce results.

The challenge for leaders and managers is often communication. Using the performance appraisal as a tool in conjunction with the strategic plan gives leaders the framework for moving their teams forward.

By operating with focus and intention on strategy you can build your business success week by week, month by month.

Chapter 14

Team Building An Essential Leadership Skill

Corporations cannot survive without teams: there's too much work to do. As a company grows it divides into teams, based on common factors. Instead of having one or several people do everything the individual employees become specialists in one aspect of the business. Companies believe this saves money and is the best way to utilize the abilities of their employees.

Dividing personnel and putting them in a certain spot on the organizational chart does not produce unity. It takes time and work to build an efficient and effective team. Unfortunately, many teams become dysfunctional. A dysfunctional team can slow productivity, service delivery and the overall operational effectiveness of the company.

Teams do not have to be dysfunctional. The leader or manager, more than anything else, determines the success or failure of a team. If the leader's agenda and delivery is all about the leader rather than the individual team members or the team, it feels like a dictatorship. This type of leader often does not want input. Employees are not confident sharing their true opinions or ideas in this type environment. Rather their responses become routine intending to please the leader. When the leader fails to do effective team building, employees do not grow, good ideas are repressed and this attitude affects all areas of their jobs and the company.

A leader not willing to listen could have their own confidence challenges as well as control problems. Many times the most qualified person for the job does not have the management and leadership skills that they need to transition to their role as leader. Leadership skills can be learned and developed. This can be accomplished through training with ongoing coaching. Unfortunately, employees are stuck with the unqualified manager while they either become more qualified as a leader or continue to operate as they have - a tough situation to be in and the company suffers.

Managing conflict in the workplace can highlight the challenges a leader can face. People fear conflict for numerous reasons. Some avoid it at all costs. This type of person is careful to make sure none of their words are interpreted as controversial. Others abandon the discussion as it starts to pick up steam. A good leader knows how to navigate conflict. Discussing different ideas and ways of doing things often leads to a better way. A good leader is comfortable facilitating diverse opinions, does not let anyone get out of order, draws out quiet employees, does not allow one person to monopolize the situation and considers all suggestions.

Leaders are expected to evaluate the performance of team members, hold them accountable, apply discipline if needed, and foster a positive team environment. A leader, who lacks self-control and does not want others to hold them accountable, finds it difficult to manage people. Team members have jobs to do, goals to reach, and expectations to meet. They grow when their manager communicates with them openly and honestly about their responsibilities. In many companies though it seems leadership styles range from one extreme to the other – they either overlook everyone's behavior or they control everything everyone does.

What can a leader do to foster healthy growth on their team? Being human and showing their vulnerability is perhaps the most important tool for good leaders. It demonstrates their authenticity, and builds trust. Many times employees feel inferior to their leaders. Therefore, they are never truly comfortable around their managers and are reluctant to speak up. A good leader admits when they are wrong as well as shares incidents to show they are imperfect humans. They make everyone feel as important as everyone else. It is difficult to build teams if employees feel favoritism exists.

A good leader encourages communication and feedback from their employees. When someone shares an idea they do not belittle that

person, and they do not let other team members attack each other. By giving each person and each idea value, the employees feel valued. When suggestions lead to positive changes, a good leader gives credit to the person with the idea as well as the team. This builds self-confidence and a strong team. Employees continue contributing. In some situations a healthy team is more productive than individuals. The team combines the strength and knowledge of all members.

A good leader keeps the team focused. In the work place, especially during meetings, it is easy to get distracted. The employees look to the manager as their example. If the manager has a negative attitude or spends too much time on personal phone calls, the employees feel this is OK. A good leader controls the work environment without being controlling. It's a common belief that actors have strong egos. Leaders lose their egos. They do not focus on their needs but rather what's best for the team. A good leader knows that without the help of their team they will not be successful. Therefore, one of their main advantages is to build a strong team.

Creating a coaching environment builds a platform for team success and effective team building. Performance Success Plans for staff can easily tie right into a team strategic plan and organizational strategic plan.

Both team and organizational strategic plans should be developed with the team that is leading them. When individual staff members buy into the company strategic plan they see their role in the success of the organization. In addition, they buy into the strategic plan because they are part of its development.

By tying the individual's success plan right to the team strategic plan goals are streamlined. When teams are meeting each month to review their strategic plan just like individuals are meeting with managers each month, communication is tremendous. One of the biggest reasons that teams fail to accomplish their goals is that there is a gap in communication. The communication gap is bridged with team meetings and individual meetings. Goals are kept in sight and the focus of work.

Chapter 15

Adjusting Your Leadership

Donna Lynn Price

*Leaders have to adjust to different employees;
different situations; and new tasks*

Leadership is one of the biggest challenges managers face. It is the challenge of how to be an effective leader that effectively motivates staff to get their jobs done and do it with the quality of an owner.

One way to look at leadership is based upon the employee and their skills, training and familiarity with the task. In this approach the leader or manager tailors their behavior as leaders to the employee's behavior.

For a new employee, the manager's behavior is very supervisory. The employee is in training mode. They need to learn the organization and the tasks that they are responsible for. The leader is more involved. The leader is in training mode; giving lots of information and direction. The goal is to develop competence and skills to a point where the leader can step back and not be as involved in the operation. Empowering employees to do their job the leader's goal.

As leaders we want our staff to be able to run with the job and not need day to day, minute by minute monitoring. This is a competent staff. The direction needed from us is minimal. The employee is able to do the job well without our direction. But, we can't just jump from directive to coach.

Although, it would be easy to have linear maps of human behavior, this again is not the case. As the manager, you will have to move easily through the different phases and be able to step back if an employee needs more direction at some point. You also will move back to directing when a new task or job duty is assigned that the employee has never done before. At this point, a new training and mentorship cycle is started and the manager's role is to provide the support needed to move successfully through each phase of developing competence to the final stage of empowered action, in which the employee is capable of doing high quality work.

Chapter 15

Building Leadership, Building Organizations

Organizations are built by teams, but the leaders are an essential key to the success of the company.

When leaders use effective leadership skills and tools such as the performance improvement system, team strategic planning and personal interaction skills of communication, taking down barriers and relationship building, they are able to empower staff to build greater and greater success. Company results soar and the work environment becomes contagious. Leaders are sought after and other departments or employees look on with envy.

Companies that invest in leadership development can see beneficial results to their entire organization. Leaders that learn to coach staff, collaborate with staffs and empower them produce higher results than leaders that over manage, control every action and don't allow staff to take action. When staffs are empowered then they can use their creativity to solve problems.

We see over and over again, when leaders talk with staff they learn more about their own organization or department. Staff sees the problems and so often the solution.

Assuming that each person wants to succeed adopting a coaching model supports leader's goals and supports staff in building their own success. By sharing in their vision, working monthly to ensure progress and overcoming obstacles managers and leaders can ensure that performance continues to move in positive directions.

What Happens When You Put Off Leadership Development?

Leadership development appears to be one of those luxury items, something that the company can live without. And it is, or is it? What happens when you have leaders that need to develop good skills and the resources are just not invested? Employees these days are not willing to work in poor work conditions. Despite the current economy and unemployment rates, employees are still willing to give up a "good job" when they feel they are treated well by managers and leaders. The cost to the company can be huge.

There is a negative impact of not addressing poor leadership, employee turnover, reduced productivity, and poor team performance. There are many potential costs to the company and impact to the bottom line. Recently, I talked with a company where this is exactly what happened. They decided to not invest in leadership development. The work environment continued to deteriorate for employees and turnover has occurred. The result: an open position on the team, lowering the ability of the team to complete jobs and meet deadlines; the need for leaders to invest time in hiring and retraining; and ultimately more loss for the company and the delay in having a fully functioning team.

Had the investment in leadership skill development been made what could the outcome have been? Higher performance of the entire team, improved work environment and culture, and reduced turnover. A stronger company and stronger bottom line result.

For many leaders or business owners, leadership skill development is viewed as a perk, a non-essential investment, but the impact of failing to make this investment can be devastating to work teams, especially when an unskilled leader or manager is involved. Some leaders have pretty natural skills, while others have never been in leadership before and have had poor role models. These folks need skill development. They need to understand their role and the impact that they have on the workforce.

When organizations do invest in leadership development positive outcomes are achieved for both the company and the individual. Leadership skill development can occur in house or via training and

executive coaching. Executive coaching helps to solidify skills once they are learned. The coach can provide feedback and additional opportunities for learning during skill acquisition and retention.

A leadership budget should take both parts of the puzzle into account. Leadership skill development and monthly executive coaching. Costs can vary from a few thousand per year ($4000) per staff person to $25,000 or more depending upon the level of training and coaching. When evaluating the investment consider the impact of the loss of just one staff person. Using the 150% of salary – just one employee leaving the organization that is a $35,000 per year employee can cost the company $52,500 in replacement and retraining costs, as well as time lost from leaders and other employees due to the shortage. The savings that could occur by investing upfront in leadership development using these numbers could be $25,000 to $48,000.

Business owners that fail to see the value of investing in leadership development for their managers and growing leaders kick themselves later when costs come back to the company.

Creating a strong leadership development program within your company is a wise investment and in the long run saves money and increases income with increased team performance and productivity.

Chapter 17

Leadership Development: Lifelong Learning

Navigating To Success:

EnVision – Evaluate – Strategic Planning – Implement – ReAssess – Leadership

Embrace a Process for Success

EnVision

Navigating a business to success takes every aspect outlined. Whether you are working with a strategic coach or a business success coach, the process remains. You MUST have a Vision. As the leader, it is up to you to envision the future – what will the company look like, feel like, be like in a year, five years, ten years or further.

Vision guides you as the leader and guides your staff and team. It is your destination. What you are striving for and it incorporates your core purpose, your mission and ultimately, becomes your navigator or compass. Your vision guides the direction of the organization and is a tool for making decisions.

Evaluate

In developing a performance culture and a successful business it is important to evaluate where you are right now. What have you accomplished? Where have you failed? What are the lessons that you have learned and that you can learn from both? These lessons can then become tools in your tool box as you build your strategies for the upcoming year.

Strategic Planning

Build your map. Your strategic plan is your map to the vision. Without a good map it is challenging to get where you want to go. Strategies can help to keep you focused, aligned and on target. It is vital to not overdo strategic planning. Keep it simple. Strategies that you can keep in front of you and keep in action.

Implementation

This is where companies fail. They create the vision, they have the strategies and then they fail to implement. Implementation gets you to the vision. Without implementation you cannot accomplish the success the company is striving for. Implementation and accountability are key.

Accountability

Building in accountability to your system or process keeps implementation going and on track. Set up a system. Score goals, report back on implementation. Have consistent meetings and accountability reports to keep each person on track and moving forward with goals and strategies.

ReAssess

Regularly you need to evaluate and reassess where you are. What strategies are working? What is not working and why? What went well? What didn't go well? What needs to improve? All of these questions are vital to keep the organization growing and improving and ultimately succeeding. Just like I have outlined throughout the book with staff, the organization needs to use a similar process of evaluation, strategic planning (performance appraisals), implementation (action plans), accountability (monthly meetings) and back to reassess and evaluate. It is a cycle of learning, a cycle of productivity and a cycle of results.

Leadership

Leadership is at the core of Navigating to Success. As the leader, you are the visionary. You drive the company. Sharing your vision and your passion is essential. It is part of leading. Bringing your staff into the fold, to KNOW the vision, collaborate on the strategies and implement builds success strategies and buy-in from your team. As the leader, you depend upon staff to bring your vision to life. It becomes essential that

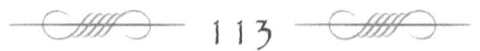

you lead. Be strategic as the leader -- develop a strategic process of navigating to success.

The process of leadership development is a cycle of continuous, lifelong learning. Leaders that choose to take on the challenge of leadership and their own personal growth and development as a leader are able to achieve more. It is a process, and an intentional one. It requires the commitment of the leader.

Most every leader is challenged in some way. Leadership is a people sport: people dynamics and when you involve people then there are challenges.

Staff will always throw unexpected curveballs for leaders to work through. Periodic assessment of skills is a great strategy for determining whether the leadership development plan has been effective in addressing the areas that needed attention. Assessment begins the cycle again. With a continuous plan for improving leadership and improving the workplace companies can achieve more than they set out to.

It begins with awareness or assessment: knowing where you are currently at. Awareness is a gift, knowing that you are not perfect, that there is room for growth and that you don't know all of the answers for interacting with your team. Completing a leadership assessment can be a tool for digging a bit deeper into your current skills. Leadership assessments can be individual or with input from constituents, such as a 360 instrument. The goal is to see where there are strengths and where there is room for growth and focused skill development. Every leader possesses some skills and every (honest) leader has areas that can improve and areas for learning and growth.

Leadership development is not just the responsibility of the company but also that of the leader. Leaders, themselves, have to recognize the need and the benefit to their leadership development. Leaders can create their own leadership development plan and review it each year. By implementing an intentional and focused leadership development plan, leaders improve the results they achieve for the businesses, their staff and teams. Investing in leadership development just makes sense.

> *Leadership Development is a lifelong process: an endeavor that takes courage and commitment, an awareness of oneself and the need to foster one's own skills.*

Chapter 19

Identifying Roles Within the Organization

Identify each role within your organization and its connection to vision

---

Vision is the path to greater success, to creating the company you want. As you identify and develop roles within the organization, be clear on how they connect to vision. Effective Communication between all staff and leaders creates an open communication system that facilitates all staff ideas being heard and valued.

Identify each role within your organization and its connection to vision also; let's take a look back at the values that you identified. What were the 6-8 values that you prioritized? We are going to be using these values as you draft your job descriptions, so it's important to revisit them here for a moment.

Next, let's look at the roles within your organization. Even within in a one person operation you have multiple roles or multiple hats that you are wearing. What are the different hats that you wear? In a larger company, what are the different roles or jobs that exist or different departments or areas? Some examples or ideas are:

Roles within your company:

1. _____

2. _____

3. _____

4. _____

POSSIBLE ROLES:

⇒ *CEO, President, Owner, Executive Director*

⇒ *Marketing Director*

⇒ *Service Provider*

⇒ *Finance Director*

⇒ *Custodian*

⇒ *Administrative/Executive Assistant*

⇒ *Sales Staff*

Roles: Connecting to Vision

Connect your vision and the roles you have identified by writing a vision statement for each role. What is the vision outcome that occurs that each role is responsible for? State it, in the present tense. This further clarifies for staff their connection to the overall vision and purpose of the organization.

Effective Communication between all staff and leaders

Create an open communication system that facilitates all staff ideas being heard and valued, I call this circles of communication. Being clear on how communication is achieved between staff and throughout the organization is important – or actually essential. When communication fails within companies the results are disastrous. It can impact all levels of functioning, clients and customers are impacted as well.

Job Descriptions

Develop job descriptions that create a positive, performance focused work environment. Even in a small company you can benefit from

defining the different roles within the company. As you grow you will already have these pieces in the plan. In developing job descriptions you clarify roles for yourself and others. Each job description has several components:

* A general statement of purpose

* Connection to the overall company vision

* Communication and how the role interfaces with other roles, customers, prospects and vendors

* Living wage statement so that we are always thinking about paying living wages for each person within our organizations: how the role is compensated

* Responsibilities: specifically what the role does on a day to day basis.

You can see that the job descriptions are connecting to the values of the organization. It builds congruity when you have your vision and values in sync and that is congruent throughout your organization.

The following job descriptions are brief outlines to give you a structure and a jumping off place to develop your organization with. Of course, it is not a comprehensive list and you will need to further develop your roles and job descriptions.

Sample job descriptions:

CEO, PRESIDENT, OWNER, FOUNDER

Is responsible for the overall health of the organization and the development of the vision.

_____

_____

Vision Outcome:

Leads the organization/company to achieve the vision. Keeps the vision in sight at all times.

_____

_____

_____

Circle of Communication:

Communicates the vision of the organization with all staff, customers and trustees or advisors. Keeps all staff and departments informed of new developments, changes, problems. Communicates with the Board of Trustees or advisors regarding organizational developments, challenges and solutions.

_____

_____

_____

Livable Wage Statement:

Earns $ _____ and works _____ hours per week, with _____ days of vacation per year and ___ paid holidays.

Responsibilities:

Works to develop the business, writing policy, recruiting new leaders for the organization, and developing new business

2. Creates a safe, effective work environment with clear operational policies.

3. Meets with business leaders and owners

4. Participates in meetings/conferences related to the core purpose of the business

5. Builds collaborative partnerships/relationships

6. Develops the vision with key leaders and staff

7. Builds the company's reputation through networking, events, serving on boards, advisory committees...

_____

_____

_____

_____

_____

_____

_____

CFO (CHIEF FINANCIAL OFFICER), FINANCE DIRECTOR, BEAN COUNTER, VICE PRESIDENT OF FINANCE, BOOK KEEPER

Oversees the financial health of the organization, monitoring income and expenses.

_____
_____
_____
_____
_____

Vision Outcome:

Keeps company financial plans in alignment with the company vision.

_____
_____
_____

Circle of Communication:

Communicates with all leadership staff; informing them consistently of the financial state of the company. Communicates with all staff responsible for purchasing; communicating with them about the company vision and how their purchasing ties into vision.

Livable Wage Statement:

Earns $ _____ and works _____ hours per week, with

_____ days of vacation per year and ____ paid holidays.

Responsibilities:

* Oversees all income and expenses

* Monitors finances weekly

* Balances Books at least monthly

* Tracks all receivables and expenses

* Completes monthly invoices

* Develops budgets with other area directors

* Works with all relevant staff to develop annual budget based on vision, values and strategic goals.

* Provides up to date information in regards to budget and actual

* Identifies trends, problems and possible solutions.

* Researches all company benefits

* Provides all financial information to accountant for taxes annually

* Communicates monthly with accountant regarding accounts

* Communicates with CEO and circle of leaders regarding financial state of the organization

* Maintains thorough financial records

* Develops financial monitoring systems and ensures they are implemented accurately.

MARKETING DIRECTOR, VICE PRESIDENT OF MARKETING, BUSINESS BUILDER

Promotes the company within the community, with prospects and with customers, in a positive, compelling manner.

_____
_____
_____

Vision Outcome:

Through the development of dynamic and vibrant marketing plans and strategies attracts the right clients and customers.

_____
_____
_____

Circle of Communication:

Listens to staff and customers/clients to gather vital information in order to promote based on vision, services/products. Provides information to staff in order to develop new services and programs based on customer/prospect needs.

_____
_____
_____

Livable Wage Statement:

Earns $ _____ and works _____ hours per week, with

_____ days of vacation per year and ___ paid holidays.

Responsibilities:

* Develops marketing and development plan

* Develops marketing plan for each marketing strategy

* Monitors effectiveness of each marketing strategy

* Develops a leads funnel based on several relevant strategies such as:

    o Networking

    o Internet: website; press releases; articles; link strategies

    o Presentations both in person and tele-class

    o Referrals

    o Advertising

    o Direct mail

    o Cold calling

    o Develops an effective marketing funnel and follow up strategy for each lead.

    o Develops annual marketing budget

    o Attends networking meetings and presentations

    o Manages leads information for all staff and tracks where each lead is the in the marketing game.

    o Writes monthly e-zine to all clients and prospects

o Implements each marketing strategy; trains appropriate staff on marketing functions: i.e., scripts for answering phones; scripts for talking with leads at networking meetings; review of presentations etc.

* Completes follow-up with each marketing effort

* Works with outside vendors to develop effective and successful marketing materials that are dynamic and vibrant

_____

_____

_____

_____

_____

DIRECTOR OF PROGRAM OPERATIONS, VICE PRESIDENT OF OPERATIONS

Provides excellent service to each client, customer, creating WOW, experiences along the way.

_____

_____

_____

_____

_____

_____

Vision Outcome:

Provides service that is excellent in delivery and outcome for clients.

_____

_____

_____

_____

_____

Circle of Communication:

Communicates with leadership circle regarding accomplishments and hurdles; new programs or new clients or changes in client status, but not client specific info.

_____

_____

_____

Livable Wage Statement:

Earns $ _____ and works _____ hours per week, with

_____ days of vacation per year and ____ paid holidays.

Responsibilities:

- ✳ Oversees and participates in daily operations

- ✳ Develops effective operational procedures with input from the operational team.

- ✳ Develops client relationships

- ✳ Orders appropriate materials for client programs

- ✳ Maximizes the use of client time

- ✳ Provides all contracts to the VP of Finance

- ✳ Delivers each program with full attention on the client and focused quality

- ✳ _____
  _____
  _____
  _____
  _____
  _____

SALES STAFF

Provides value to contacts, prospects and customers throughout the sales process.

_____

_____

_____

_____

_____

_____

Vision Outcome:

Provides value to each prospect, building long lasting relationships.

_____

_____

_____

_____

_____

_____

Circle of Communication:

Communicates with leadership circle the status of prospects, leads, lost sales and closed sales, highlighting accomplishments and challenges. Communicates openly and honestly with potential customers/clients.

_____

_____

_____

Livable Wage Statement:

Earns $ _____ and works _____ hours per week, with

_____ days of vacation per year and ___ paid holidays.

Responsibilities:

- Documents each sale, contract and agreement

- Provides detailed outline of service to program/service delivery staff, finance, and client before work ensues.

- Ensures enough lead time for operations to gather needed resources to plan work and implement service effectively

_____

_____

_____

_____

_____

ADMINISTRATIVE EXECUTIVE, VIRTUAL ASSISTANT, EXECUTIVE ASSISTANT

Keeps the place running smoothly: knows all operations and how they work. Interfaces with all staff as required.

_____
_____
_____
_____
_____
_____

Vision Outcome:

Builds relationships with clients, customers, prospects, vendors and the leadership circle as well as all staff.

_____
_____
_____
_____
_____

Circle of Communication:

Communicates with the leadership circle regarding vital data of the organization.

_____
_____
_____
_____

Livable Wage Statement:

Earns $ _____ and works _____ hours per week, with

_____ days of vacation per year and ___ paid holidays.

Responsibilities:

* Manages the vital data of the organization:

* Customer information

* Lead information

* Vendors

* Other Contacts

* Enters new contacts into the database and links with appropriate auto mail such as e-zine; e-course, etc.

* Schedules meetings/appointments with each new lead per policy

* Is the first contact for customers, clients, prospects, vendors and colleagues, presents the organization in the very best way.

* Monitors the auto-responder program for each marketing effort

* Coordinates the referral thank you program

* Enters financial data into the accounting system

* Assists with the monthly e-zine

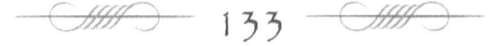

Chapter 18:

Managing and Navigating Change

New Opportunities in a New Environment

Creating a coaching environment shifts the entire workplace. Leadership development is happening, staff are motivated and inspired, and the environment is bubbling with new results. This creates an inspirational workplace that begins creating new opportunities. The entire workplace is in the flow of positive energy. That flow is the energy of creativity. It is contagious and infectious, just as negative workplaces are, but this is so much better!

The shift in the workplace is worth making but as discussed it takes some things to make it happen. It also takes ongoing keys for success to maintain the positive changes.

Commitment:

Leaders and managers must be fully committed to the change. If not, the new approach will fail. Coaching will be seen as ineffective when in reality it was the lack of commitment and follow through that failed. Initially, there was a commitment to making the shift, now the changes have occurred. Leaders have to stay the course. Staff will try to shift back. Even if the previous environment was poor, it was familiar. Unbelievably, good energy and good changes can still feel scary and unfamiliar.

Leaders have to continue to reinforce the changes that have occurred and keep the focused performance success plans moving forward. Staff will begin to let the monthly accountability meetings slide, day to day priorities will interfere. Leaders must reinforce that these meetings are keys to the coaching environment and must continue to happen. They are priority.

Full Implementation:

Coaching cannot just happen with frontline staff; it must happen at all levels of the organization. Holding just frontline staff accountable creates a double standard that is seen and impacts the performance throughout the company. This goes back to commitment. If the company is fully committed then the leaders are coaching and being coached. Just like staff each leader has a performance success plan that outlines their top goals for the year that are tied into the company vision and strategy. Leaders are reviewing their plans monthly and making changes to their performance to meet their goals.

Open Communication

In building a coaching organization, you are opening communication. The leaders are asking for staff to communicate, to give input and receive feedback. Leaders have to be willing to do this as well. Communicating throughout the shifting environment is vital. What's working, what's not working, where do we still need to focus? Asking questions throughout the process, hearing the feedback gives the leaders information about navigating change.

Continuous Learning

A thriving organization is one that is continuing to learn and grow. The coaching approach facilitates this and enables and empowers staff and leaders to do just that.

Appendix 1:
ICF Coaching Core
Competencies

International Coaches Federation

The following eleven core coaching competencies were developed to support greater understanding about the skills and approaches used within today's coaching profession as defined by the ICF. They will also support you in calibrating the level of alignment between the coach-specific training expected and the training you have experienced.

Finally, these competencies were used as the foundation for the ICF Credentialing process examination. The core competencies are grouped into four clusters according to those that fit together logically based on common ways of looking at the competencies in each group. The groupings and individual competencies are not weighted - they do not represent any kind of priority in that they are all core or critical for any competent coach to demonstrate.

A. SETTING THE FOUNDATION
1. MEETING ETHICAL GUIDELINES AND PROFESSIONAL STANDARDS
2. ESTABLISHING THE COACHING AGREEMENT

B. CO-CREATING THE RELATIONSHIP
3. ESTABLISHING TRUST AND INTIMACY WITH THE CLIENT
4. COACHING PRESENCE

C. COMMUNICATING EFFECTIVELY
5. ACTIVE LISTENING

6. POWERFUL QUESTIONING
7. DIRECT COMMUNICATION

D. FACILITATING LEARNING AND RESULTS
8. CREATING AWARENESS
9. DESIGNING ACTIONS
10. PLANNING AND GOAL SETTING
11. MANAGING PROGRESS AND ACCOUNTABILITY

(International Coaches Federation (ICF) 2011
http://coachfederation.org/icfcredentials/core-competencies/)

Appendix 2: Resources

The Performance Improvement System:

Compass Rose Consulting provides a powerful and simple performance improvement system for organizations. Using the Best Year Yet® system for team strategic planning and company performance success plans we have found tremendous success and results. Best Year Yet® has been used effectively with corporate teams, non-profit organizations, individuals and businesses for over 30 years and it has consistently produced results for those that use it. Using a simple performance success plan tool facilitates the coaching experience for staff and makes the entire system work more effectively for the business.

Pick up a copy of our information packet at: **www.performanceimprovementsystem.com**

Leadership and Team Assessments:

Leadership Assessments: We offer a comprehensive leadership assessment, either personal assessment or full 360 assessment.

Team Assessments:

Assess the functioning of your team. Is it functional or dysfunctional? Where is the dysfunction? Let us teach you strategies to overcome the dysfunctions.

Schedule your consult to review your assessment needs.

Employee Coaching for Business Success Training Programs:

Imagine....staff that is inspired, motivated, and working hard to produce results for you.....

If you are business owner with staff then your business results depend on your ability to work in partnership with your staff. Their loyalty and commitment to your business increases your results and ultimately your bottom line. But employee relationships are among the most difficult. There's an unwritten "we" versus "them" mentality that exists even when the owner works to not have that. Employee Coaching for Business Success gives you the framework for building an effective partnership with your staff and the skills to coach them for success (both yours and theirs).

Employee Coaching for Business Success is designed to give you the skills and the framework for coaching your staff, building them up and helping them to achieve their vision as well as yours.

This five session (virtual) or full day training program is packed full of skill development information for your managers and for you. You will learn the skills you need to change your work environment and make it one that is highly productive.

As a manager and supervisor for many years I tried to "coach" staff but I didn't have the complete picture of what those skills are or know how to create the environment to make it all work. Working with poor performers is frustrating. As frustration builds performance often gets worse instead of better. I have lived through that frustration. I have seen teams frustrated and staff under-performing. After training as a coach, I found the skills that managers and business owners need to really create the work environment that most of us are striving for. I had the skills

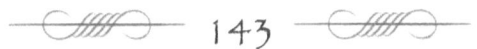

and I used some of them as a manager but now this program puts them all together for you. And, I coach you to be a successful coach yourself.

You will learn - the fundamental coaching skills every manager needs to know and use to guarantee their results

You will learn - coaching skills that enhance the performance of your staff and help you to create a partnership with them that is focused on success and results. (Benefiting your bottom line results)

You will learn - how to use your annual performance appraisal as a positive meeting for enhancing employee performance and change the framework of the performance appraisal to one that is employee focused and builds on success.

You will learn to - create an instant rapport and "tune-in" to your staff so that you know what is happening in the workplace and can make changes as needed. Staffs have a wealth of knowledge for you about what is working and what isn't working; you want that knowledge and that rapport with staff.

You will learn how to - co-create a partnership and vision for you and your employee that enhances their productivity, attitude and performance.

You will build - a trusting relationship with each staff member, so that they are working harder for you.

You will learn - new tools to give staff to prosper and thrive to build staff.

The real benefits to you as the owner or manager are:

* results that your team will produce for you after you master these coaching skills. You will see

* increases in productivity

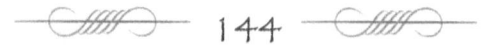

* improved performance

* decreases in absenteeism & staff turnover

* a shift in culture to one of loyalty and commitment.

You will feel better about your meetings with staff.

You will sleep at night because you know that you are providing a great work environment and you are creating a successful business.

Ultimately, your job will become easier because you will know that you have dedicated, qualified, competent staff working for you.

Employee Coaching for Business Success gives you the skills you need AND from the comfort of your home or office. There are no travel expenses, no travel time, no time away from your business or family!

Employee Coaching for Business Success will teach you the skills you need to work more effectively with your staff. Do your staffs not treat your business with as much passion as you do? Are you trying to achieve something that staffs just aren't on board with? Learn the skills to shift the culture to a performance culture that is passionate about the company vision & achieving it.

You will learn practical, usable coaching skills. You will have the chance to practice these skills, ask questions, and get feedback. Each class is packed full of information. We provide you with:

Class Materials:

* Donna's new book: "Employee Coaching for Success"

* Five 90 Minute Video Conference Classes with recording link for each call available within 48 hours following the class.

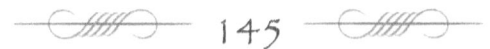

* One on-line subscription to the Performance Improvement System we use in our coaching programs (Value $199) Additional subscriptions are available for other team members.

* Personal Coaching Session ($250 Value). You will receive one personal coaching session. During this one hour session you will have the opportunity to develop your personal skills, create your personal plan for implementing the material you have learned in the class and ask any questions you have that you felt you couldn't ask during the class. This coaching session really gives you the chance to put this material into practice in your unique setting, with the help of a professional coach.

* Online Group to Discuss Class Materials with other participants In addition to Donna participating in the email group, other participants can also respond to your questions, challenges and successes. The value of a group is tremendous. The group brings with it tremendous experience and insight. You benefit from all of that when you join the group and participate.

Your business is your passion; its success your ultimate goal. You are depending on your staff to help to get you there. If you don't use effective coaching skills in building your staff and supporting their success, ultimately your business fails. Join Employee Coaching for Business Success to build your skills and your success. You can't afford to have staffs that aren't performing for you. You can't afford to wait to develop your effective coaching skills. If you wait, you continue to lose money, clients, sales......Don't wait any longer. Invest in yourself and your business.

Course Outline:

1. Creating the Framework for Using Coaching

Learn critical strategies for creating a coaching environment. How to shift the workplace culture to a performance focused environment, coaching and empowerment.

2. Communicating Effectively, Active Listening, Powerful Questioning, Direct Communication

Powerful Questions, Observations and Requests How to think, language, and ask powerful questions, make powerful requests.

3. Juggling Managing and Coaching

As a manager there are times when you move back into a management role and shift out of coaching to an extent. In this session we will review how to juggle, management, supervision, discipline and coaching. Learn how to make it work.

4. Using an Effective Performance Improvement Tool.

Learn how to integrate coaching into the performance appraisal tool and make the appraisal into a success plan that employees embrace and strive to master.

5. Ongoing Coaching, Shifting the Work Culture.

Keeping the plan alive and focused. In this class we will review how to keep the employee's plan alive but also how to keep the new shift in work culture positive and motivating.

ABOUT THE AUTHOR

Donna Price, strategic team builder and business success coach specializes in working with business leaders and their teams to create powerful strategic plans, build effective and high performing teams and create a work place culture that is healthy and thriving. Donna has 18+ years mid and upper level management experience; supervising multiple teams and managers; growing programs from $750,000 to $2+ million in program operations and increasing staff teams under her management from two teams to more than 12 teams. Her experience includes developing residential options for people with disabilities and being director of an experiential outdoor education center and summer camp for underserved urban youth. She has been successful in program development, policy and procedure development, staff training and program certification and accreditation. She has worked to guide programs to be sustainable work places that are life nurturing and enriching.

Donna founded her company Compass Rose Consulting in 2003 providing services to small business owners, business leaders and teams. Donna brings a unique background in facilitation, coaching, team building and adventure education to her work. She brings all of her skills together to help in building the most effective programs and solutions for clients. By using customized facilitation and coaching approaches

Donna Lynn Price

Donna through her partnerships with business leaders is able to guide shifts in work place culture to high performing; facilitate team development and strategic planning.

Donna lives in rural northwest New Jersey with her partner, Ken and their two daughters. They cycle frequently on tandems, touring with all of their gear, and kayak with their dog. They love family time and outdoor adventure.

Donna can be reached at her company:

www.CompassRoseConsulting.com

dprice@compassroseconsulting.com

973-948-7673